INFORMATION:
THE ULTIMATE MANAGEMENT RESOURCE

Information:
The Ultimate Management Resource

HOW TO FIND, USE, AND MANAGE IT

Morton F. Meltzer

A DIVISION OF AMERICAN MANAGEMENT ASSOCIATIONS

Dedicated to
DAVID AND BARBARA MELTZER
and their two children
ELISABETH AND NORMAN

Library of Congress Cataloging in Publication Data

Meltzer, Morton F.
    Information, the ultimate management resource.

    Bibliography: p.
    Includes index.
    1. Management information systems.   I. Title.
T58.6.M473   658.4'038   81-66222
ISBN 0-8144-5700-2   AACR2

© 1981 AMACOM
A division of American Management Associations, New York.
All rights reserved.
Printed in the United States of America.

Second Printing

Preface

Information is the manager's main tool, indeed the manager's "capital," and it is he who must decide what information he needs and how to use it.[1]

—Peter F. Drucker

Today's managers must learn to cope with increasingly complex demands placed upon them in the Age of Information. Where can managers get timely, accurate, reliable information? How can managers minimize their information-related needs in decision making? What are the power payoffs and costs that result from information systems? Who are the information managers? These questions are vital to a manager's career and an organization's well being, and this book helps answer them.

Another purpose of this book is to alert business, industry, and government to the necessity of treating information as a valuable resource. Information is not free. It is a commodity that must be managed. How can managers of organizations plan, budget, and audit their information resources? What organizational structure is needed to manage information efficiently and effectively in the corporation? Where do the information managers belong on the organization charts? What new technologies and services are needed to

1. Peter F. Drucker, "Managing the Information Explosion," *The Wall Street Journal,* April 10, 1980, p. 24, cols. 4–6.

compete in this information-intensive society? What is the impact of information on motivation and productivity? This book provides answers to the critical questions that managers of private and public sector organizations must resolve.

Part I, "The Informed Manager," tells how information affects the manager's role. The first chapter establishes a background against which to understand the new responsibilities and challenges that managers face in the Age of Information. A synthesis of management concepts and principles provides the reader with a new insight for successful management. Chapter 2 deals with the payoffs and costs of information power, shows the strategies and tactics of information power, explains how to cope with information overload, and describes how information relates to motivation and productivity. The paperless office of the future is here, and Chapter 3 looks at information technology as a management tool. Communications, computer, and audiovisual technologies combine to create the electronic office and the corporate war room in which you must be able to function. You must learn how to use these electronic aids to improve yourself and preserve your organization's well-being. Chapter 4 presents and describes various sources of information available to the manager, both from within the organization and from outside services. The structure of the information industry is analyzed to help the manager better determine how and when to use information brokers, to make or buy information systems, and to be electronically retrieve information cost effectively.

Part II, "Manageable Information," looks at information as a valuable commodity. Chapter 5 sees information as a personal, organizational, and natural resource that has a price tag and intrinsic value. Resource sharing through technology transfer, trade associations, and clearinghouses are considered. Protecting information through copyrights, patents, trade secrets, proprietary rights, and electronic safeguards are covered in detail. Chapter 6 offers several methods that can be used as guides to plan, budget, and audit the information resources of the organization. The economics of information are further studied in Chapter 7, which deals with managing information throughout its life cycle.

Part III, "The Information Manager," introduces a new management concept with respect to the organization chart. Chapter 8 suggests various organizational structures to consider in establishing an information manager's slot in the organization. Chapter 9 outlines career guidelines for those who want to become information managers in business, industry, and government. Chapter 10 takes a broad perspective of information management and addresses the various roles of an information manager in the context of such critical issues as organizational and personal privacy and government disclosures. Chapter 11 provides you with a series of management doctrines and principles to guide you and your organization in achieving your goals and extending your reach in the Age of Information.

Part IV closes the book with an information source book to help you locate resources.

This book looks at managers in a new work environment—an information milieu—and addresses the real-world problems that have accompanied the new environment's arrival. The emergence of information resource managers working for both private gain and public good in business and government will make a major impact on how society develops economically, politically, and socially in the years to come. Managers and government executives must reassess their own roles and decide which direction their organizations will move in light of the developments described here.

Morton F. Meltzer

Acknowledgments

As original as this book is, it is the result of the evolution of management concepts during my years of practical work in the fields of information and communication. I have been privileged to exchange ideas with my professional colleagues, and you will share many of these ideas as you read this book. Thus, I want to acknowledge those individuals who encouraged me to write this book and who critically reviewed its contents in various stages of development.

Top management at Martin Marietta Corporation recognizes information as a corporate resource and has created a supportive environment in which to work. Specifically, Robert J. Whalen, President of the Aerospace Orlando Division; W. Hugh Parks, Jr., Vice President and General Manager, Development Division; John S. Bright, Director of Product Support/Logistics; and David M. McLean, Manager of Presentations, have supported and promoted the information center's activities to improve and expand information resources and services. The entire staff at the information center has shown great flexibility in accepting and implementing many of the ideas set forth here.

Paul G. Zurkowski, President of the Information Industry Association, and Dr. Gary Robinson of System Development Corporation reviewed the narrative outline of this book and made constructive comments. Ann C. Mann edited the draft copy of the manuscript with skill and understanding. Sharon L. Bowker typed and retyped my original manuscript with patience and understanding. AMACOM's planning and acquisition editor, Thomas Gannon, provided suggestions to make the book beneficial to all managers who must cope with the new challenges of the Age of Information.

Contents

Part I:
The Informed Manager

1

SETTING AND SYNTHESIS

*Numerous studies have documented that the U.S. has been
in the throes of an historic transition for the past two decades. The old industrial society that generated wealth in
the form of capital goods and manufactured products is
giving way to a new society valued in terms of intangible
assets, such as knowledge and information processing.*[1]
—Business Week, *June 30, 1980*

You, as a manager, now operate in a new economic, political, and
social environment. The U.S. economy has shifted from an industrial base to an information base. Thus, you must acquire new skills,
formulate definitive policies for your organization, and assume
greater responsibilities to cope with the information setting into
which you have been thrust. It is vital for you to recognize and deal
with these new realities in the business, government, and private
nonprofit sectors.

INFORMATION ENVIRONMENT

The change in the economy from an industrial base to an information base had been predicted and is well documented. In 1977,
the U.S. Department of Commerce issued an extensive nine-volume
report titled *The Information Economy,* which shows that 46 percent
of the Gross National Product is linked to information-related activity, and that nearly half the labor force works at some sort of information-related job, earning 53 percent of labor income. The
transformation of the United States from an agricultural, through

3

an industrial, to an information-based society is a reality in which you are working. An earlier study by economist Fritz Machlup, *The Production and Distribution of Knowledge in the United States,* published in 1962 by Princeton University Press, estimated that as much as 29 percent of the Gross National Product was tied up with the production, processing, and distribution of information.

Even before the federal government provided statistical evidence substantiating the emergence of today's information-based society, voices from academia, industry, and government had predicted the evolution—and it now affects every American.

In 1964, Peter F. Drucker wrote,

> Other resources, money or physical equipment, for instance, do not confer any distinction. What does make a business distinct and what is its peculiar resource is its ability to use knowledge of all kinds—from scientific and technical knowledge to social, economic, and managerial knowledge. It is only in respect to knowledge that a business can be distinct, can therefore produce something that has a value in the market place.[2]

Zbigniew Brzezinski, former national security adviser, predicted in *Between Two Ages: America's Role in the Technetronic Era* that:

> Today, the most industrially advanced countries (in the first instance, the United States) are beginning to emerge from the industrial stage of their development. They are entering an age in which technology and especially electronics—hence my neologism "technetronic"—are increasingly becoming the principal determinants of social change, altering the mores, the social structure, the values, and the global outlook of society.[3]

Daniel Bell encompassed his forecast in the title of his opus, *The Coming of Post-Industrial Society* (1973). He explained that the post-industrial society involves five dimensions: (1) the transformation to a service economy, (2) the ascendancy of the professional and technical class, (3) the dominance of theoretical knowledge as the mainspring of innovation and of policy making for the society, (4) the control of technology and technological assessment, and (5) the development of a new "intellectual technology" for decision making. In a talk to the American Institute of Physics, Bell later defined the post-industrial society as basically an information-based society.

In 1974 the American Academy of Political and Social Science published a special edition of its *Annals,* entitled "The Information Revolution." The following year the American Society of Public Administration addressed the subject in a "Symposium on Knowledge Management" published in *Public Administration Review.* Other business and social commentators and professional societies have referred to this phenomenon using similar terms, all of which can be described by the broad phrase, the Age of Information.

IMPLICATIONS FOR MANAGEMENT

What are the implications of the Age of Information for management? From one perspectivve, every individual, from the chief executive officer to the first-line supervisor, is a manager of information. Likewise, in the public sector, every person in the entire spectrum of management is an administrator of information. If, as studies have revealed, 75 percent of the average manager's time is spent communicating, then each one is indeed a manager of information.

From another point of view, the demands for information placed upon today's management structure mandate the establishment of an information manager within the hierarchy of the organization. Economic, technological, and social impacts on information have accelerated and expanded with exponential velocity and magnitude. As a result, the astute organization manager recognizes that a focal point is needed to cope with the problems of information, both internally and externally. The solution is to make one person responsible for the coordination of the information resources and requirements of the organization. That person is the information manager.

However, with the emergence of the information manager, the managers of personnel, finance, production, materials, and facilities take on added dimensions in today's information-based society. Within the organization there are constant demands for timely, accurate information to assess past program performance, current organizational functions, and future opportunities and options. And outside the organization, regulatory agencies, customers, vendors, professional groups, and others require information to fulfill legislated obligations, evaluate ideas, and make decisions.

In addition, the risks accompanying increased information management must be considered. Failing to manage information or mismanaging it can cut into an organization's profits by increasing operating expenses. Some of the direct results of mismanaged information are duplication of effort, decisions based on outdated or erroneous information, decreased productivity, and loss of market influence.

The effects on an organization's human resources should not be overlooked. Too often we explain away personnel problems with the glib phrase, "a breakdown in communication." But lack of communication within an organization and the psychological burden that results are frequently caused by the loss of information. Also to be considered is the loss of information that occurs when a key executive or chief research scientist leaves the organization. What contigency plans have been made and what insurance is provided for such a brain drain from your company?

Principles of management are another major consideration. Are the management guidelines of a labor-oriented era applicable to an information-intensive society? It is important for managers to realize that an information doctrine must be developed, not to replace or displace current management philosophy, but to supplement existing concepts. An information orientation should be superimposed on the management of a private enterprise, government agency, or philanthropic association.

Because many people associate technology, specifically the computer, with the Age of Information, managers may see the evolving organizational setting as less people-oriented and more machine-based. The current literature abounds in such terms as "man–machine interface" and "artificial intelligence," used to connote the near-exclusion of humans from the paperless office. This depersonalized description is popular but specious. The need for improved personnel relations is imperative in the Age of Information. The people-oriented management philosophies of Henri Fayol, Frederick W. Taylor, Mary Parker Follett, Chester I. Barnard, Douglas McGregor, and others provide a firm foundation upon which wise managers can construct principles and practices directly related to the Age of Information.

HIERARCHY OF TERMS

The Age of Information has brought with it a new body of terminology that may confuse today's managers. The clarification of such terms as data, information, intelligence, and knowledge is necessary before managers can understand their expanded roles as both producers and users of information within an organization.

Data are basic facts and figures. The cost of raw materials, the gross sales of a corporation, the number of clients, and the rate of production are all examples of data. Data are descriptive rather than evaluative.

Information is the result of the analysis, synthesis, and evaluation based on available data. Examples of information are "The cost of a raw material will probably increase because of a supply shortage," "Sales are down due to a competitive product line that has taken over a significant share of the market," "The number of clients can be increased by offering additional service," and "The rate of production will stabilize over the next six months as a result of automation."

According to the U.S. Department of Commerce, "Information is data that have been organized and communicated. The information *activity* includes all the resources consumed in producing, processing, and distributing information goods and services."[4]

Disinformation is distorted or false information disseminated with the intention of misleading the listener or reader. The word is a translation of the Russian word *dezinformatsiya,* which is used as part of the title of a branch of the Soviet secret service whose purpose is to deceive foreign intelligence agents.

Intelligence refers to information that relates to policy decisions. The term is usually used in the private sector in the fields of marketing and planning. In the public sector, intelligence is frequently defined as information about an enemy or potential enemy. The CIA and information-gathering agencies of the State and Defense Departments are identified with this aspect of intelligence in the public's mind. Political, economic, and social information, as well as data on quantities of resources and hardware, are categorized under this term.

Knowledge is related to learning and academia. Usually it refers to what an organization or person knows or can know about a particular subject. Knowledge is information put to use. The so-called "knowledge" industries are those that supply the academic world with information: the libraries, schools, colleges, and universities that provide education and the mass media that supply information to the general public.

The adjectives *soft* and *hard* are frequently used in conjunction with the terms data, information, intelligence, and knowledge. "Soft" indicates information whose value and reliability are questionable because of the source or ambiguity of evidence. "Hard" refers to information that is valid and can be used with a high degree of confidence in making decisions.

Harry Levinson, a clinical psychologist and president of the Levinson Institute in Cambridge, Massachusetts, is a consultant to business and industry. In 1977 he delineated the difference between information and data in an interview with *Psychology Today.* Referring to his efforts in setting up and heading a division of industrial mental health for the Menninger Foundation, Levinson recalled,

> Those were the days before anyone had ever heard of community psychiatry. We were completely in the dark. I spent 18 months following my nose around the country, talking to those few psychologists in industry, to executives, to anyone concerned with the mental health of working adults. I found there were lots of data but no information. Nothing you could apply to real problems.[5]

And the Nobel-prize-winning poet T. S. Eliot philosophically questioned the descending hierarchy of terms in his 1934 poem, *The Rock.*

Where is the wisdom we have lost in knowledge?
Where is the knowledge we have lost in information?[6]

TYPES OF INFORMATION SYSTEMS

Managers and administrators entering business and government today will have to deal with some type of information system. So will young executives on their way up the corporate ladder. "Old pros" will have to adjust to the advent of the information systems within their own organizations.

A popular misconception about information systems is that all of them are computerized. Admittedly, most of the sophisticated systems rely on computers because computers have the capability of storing, manipulating, and retrieving a large volume of information. However, many useful information systems are not computerized. The ultimate test of a good information system is not the extent of mechanization or the size, but rather the accuracy of the information in the system and, most importantly, how well you, the manager, can use the stored information for planning, managing, and evaluating programs.

There are many types of information systems, including management, marketing, scientific and technical, urban, medical, and legal information systems. The basic concept of all types of systems remains the same.

The management information system (MIS) evolved within the business community in response to the development of computer systems, the advances in communications technology, and the growth of systems techniques. The MIS collects, merges, and stores information in a common data base. Management may interact with and extract information from this MIS in any desired detail or format.

Three major subsystems make up the MIS. The *operating subsystem* is composed of data that are used in everyday business operations. Production and inventory controls, payrolls, and billings are typical elements. The *reporting subsystem* provides management reports that may or may not be derived from the operating subsystem. Reports giving the number of sales may spin off from the operating subsystem; the breakdown of a competitor's financial situation might be introduced independently for later retrieval. The *decision-making subsystem* is the third category of the MIS. This subsystem offers managers information that will help them decide among various alternative courses of action. Mathematical models and simulations are included in this subsystem.

Marketing information systems contain data that managers can use to help them choose a product, determine its price, distribution, and promotion, and conduct marketing research that will enable them to assess the success of the current marketing mix and suggest future endeavors.

Scientific and technical information systems are primarily organized for information storage and retrieval. Most systems are based on traditional abstracting and indexing services whose purpose is to locate a document that covers a particular subject. Modern systems provide factual information and full text retrieval in addition to bibliographic references.

Urban information systems provide public administrators with information about such government functions as transportation, criminal justice, social services, public finance, and economic development. Thus, urban or municipal information systems that have the same range as management information systems can be used to conduct simple billings for utilities, to prepare payrolls, and to provide city and county administrators with information for major planning and policy decisions.

Medical information systems provide services that range from carrying out basic housekeeping functions such as patient billings, hospital inventory, and payrolls to maintaining medical records, diagnosing illnesses, and, in some instances, recommending therapeutic procedures.

Lawyers and lawmakers have access to information systems that are comparable to scientific and technical systems. Congressmen can find out the status of bills and resolutions or link into the Library of Congress for briefs on vital issues. A computer terminal also helps their constituents to locate applicable federal loans and grants. Lawyers can search a national law library covering decisions of the U.S. Supreme Court, Circuit Courts, and District Courts and can gain access to the complete current version of the U.S. Code. The point is that you, a manager in business, industry, or government, must learn how to gain access to these information systems and put them to use to achieve your organization's goals and further your own career. Managing in the Age of Information mandates a cerebral, not a visceral or mechanistic, approach to problem solving and decision making. The manager who has command of the intellectual tools at his disposal will be the hero of the success story of the next generation.

REFERENCES

1. "Technology Gives the U.S. a Big Edge," *Business Week,* June 30, 1980, p. 102.
2. Peter F. Drucker, *Managing for Results* (New York: Harper & Row, 1964), p. 5.
3. Zbigniew Brzezinski, *Between Two Ages: America's Role in the Technetronic Era* (New York: Viking, 1970), p. *xiv*.
4. Marc Uri Porat, *The Information Economy: Definition and Measurement,* U.S. Department of Commerce, Office of Telecommunications, OT Special Publication 77-12(1) (Washington, D.C.: Government Printing Office, May 1977), p. 2.
5. Daniel Goleman, "The Levinson Treatment for Industrial Complexes," *Psychology Today,* December 1977, p. 48. © 1977 Ziff Davis Publishing Co. Reprinted with permission.
6. T. S. Eliot, "Choruses from 'The Rock'," in *Collected Poems 1909-1962* (New York: Harcourt Brace, 1963), p. 147. By permission of publisher.

2

PAYOFFS AND COSTS OF INFORMATION POWER

How significant was the Information Revolution of the mid-1980s? It enriched the minds of consumers, gave them more leisure time, and raised their standard of living.

For businesses and workers, however, it was a mixed blessing. The winners were not, for the most part, merely lucky. Back in the late 1970s they saw the revolution coming and prepared themselves by forecasting its impact on their organizations and taking the appropriate exploitative (or evasive) action. The losers ignored or scoffed at the impending changes and perhaps never saw what hit them.[1]

—Harvey L. Poppel

You and all the other individuals within your organization who make decisions, solve problems, and stimulate creativity need information to perform your tasks and fulfill your responsibilities. This is true at all levels of management—information in today's Age of Information is a primary need.

USES OF INFORMATION POWER

Information power is used to accomplish four basic goals: to inform, to influence, to innovate, and to evaluate. In each case, information is used both actively and passively. You want to inform others—and be informed yourself. You want to issue directives, instruct personnel, and communicate items of interest, but you also need to be informed about the status of your operations, the current economic trends, and the latest regulations affecting your business or agency. Besides wanting to influence the decisions of others, you also want to be persuaded with various ideas and concepts. New products and services and original marketing methods originate from an innovative organization, whether it is a research and development laboratory or a Madison Avenue advertising agency. As a manager your responsibility is to spark others to come up with new ideas. You also need to be prompted to think creatively yourself. Judgments are integral to the management responsibility, and you need information to evaluate your different options, and in turn, you will want to have your suggestions evaluated in the proper informational context.

These four uses of information power are not mutually exclusive. They may be used in concert with each other in pursuit of your objectives. At the same time that you are informing another person you may also be influencing the individual; you may possibly give the person a new insight into possible creative solutions. Conversely, this interaction may also allow the man or woman to evaluate better a situation with new information.

Information can also be abused: disinformation may be used to intentionally mislead. You may wince at the thought and question the objective on ethical, moral, and legal grounds, but the realities or organizational life dictate that you must be aware that information may be used in this way to confound you.

SOURCES OF POWER

You derive power in five possible ways: through legitimate authority, charisma, knowledge, ability to reward, and ability to punish.

Legitimate power comes to you from your place in the organization's hierarchy. If the position you hold in your company is recognized as a seat of authority, then your office and the information it produces have a high degree of influence on others. The credibility factor increases significantly when information is issued from a respected position of authority. It is important to note that authority by itself does not automatically command respect or credibility.

Saul Alinsky, the community organizer, recalled an incident

from his youth that illustrates how easily an authoritative relationship can crumble.

> It wasn't defiance so much as curiosity in action, which seems to others to be defiance. My father, for example: he was far from permissive and I'd get my share of beatings, with the invariable finale, "You ever do that again and you know what's going to happen to you!" I'd just nod, sniffling, and skulk away. But finally one day, after he'd really laid into me, he stood over me swinging his razor strap and repeated, "You know what's going to happen to you if you do that again?" and I just said through my tears, "No, what's going to happen?" His jaw dropped open, he was completely at a loss, he didn't know what the hell to say. He was absolutely disorganized. I learned my lesson then: Power is not in what the establishment has but in what you *think* it has.[2]

A similar challenge to authority took place at the White House. According to John Dean's testimony before the Senate Watergate Committee:

> The President told me that he had been thinking about this entire matter and thought it might be a good idea if he had in his drawer a letter from me requesting that he accept my resignation or in the alternative an indefinite leave of absence. He said that he had prepared two letters for my signature and he would not do anything with them at this time but thought it would be good if he had them.
> He then passed me a manila file folder with two letters in them. The President said that he had prepared the letters himself and that no one would know I had signed them. I read the letters and was amazed at what I was being asked to sign. . . . The first letter, dated April 16, 1973, read . . .
> "In view of my increasing involvement in the Watergate matter, my impending appearance before the grand jury, and the probability of its action, I request an immediate and indefinite leave of absence from my position on your staff."
> The second letter, which was even more incriminating, read . . .
> "As a result of my involvement in the Watergate matter, which we discussed last night and today, I tender you my resignation effective at once."
> After reading the letters, I looked the President squarely in the eyes and told him that I could not sign the letters. He was annoyed with me and somewhat at a loss for words.[3]

Power achieved through charisma is based not upon position within the organization, but rather upon how others see the person involved as one who is liked and with whom others like to associate. *Charisma* is the power to lead people and arouse their loyalty and enthusiasm. The charismatic leader provides people with information that will be useful to them even though he may not be the originator of that information and is not legitimately authorized or responsible for providing the information. But because he fulfills the information needs of others voluntarily he builds up a power base that may be more influential than that of the person who is designated a leadership role.

The person who is seen by others as a knowledgeable person in a particular area has "expert power" at his disposal. As our society becomes more technocratic and specialized, the influential role of the expert has increasing impact. The power and prestige of experts have grown to such an extent that some sociologists refer to expertocracy. As the late Supreme Court Justice William O. Douglas warned, ". . . the experts have so multiplied that man has a new sense of impotence; man is indeed about to be delivered to them."[4] Expert power is not limited to social, scientific, and technical disciplines, but includes knowledge of where to get information and knowing how the system operates in order to get what is wanted. The power of many Washington insiders emanates from their knowledge of sources of information and from knowing who pulls the levers of power within government. SRI International futurologist Peter Schwartz says, "What we are doing is creating a new class structure around wealth—this time the wealth of information. Like today's 'haves and have-nots,' we will be a society of the 'knows and know-nots.' "[5]

The power of reward is based upon a person's ability to confer psychological or financial rewards on others. People have needs they want fulfilled. How well these needs can be gratified is directly proportional to the power a person holds over his subordinates, peers, and even superiors. People need information. Anyone who can fill that need acquires power within your organization.

The extent to which others perceive one person as possessing the power to penalize or hurt them determines that person's power.

Punishment need not be restricted to an economic arena, involving demotions and job loss, but may be expanded to include psychological aspects. For example people need to be kept informed and may be punished by not being provided with information they expressly need or want.

In essence, the power of information is the common denominator of each one of these five sources of power. Information permeates all of them. These power techniques may be used independently or)in combination. Today's managers must have a sense of timing— they must know when it is appropriate to draw on sources of information power and how to combine sources to achieve their goals. Information power is muscle. Just as athletes must exercise to avoid flabbiness and stay in physical shape, mentally fit managers must flex their "information muscles" to be effective and be recognized by their subordinates, peers and superiors as people with power and influence within their organization.

Rosabeth Moss Kanter, author of *Men and Women of the Corporation,* addresses the subject of productive power in a *Harvard Business Review* article. She maintains that power is derived from three sources. First, a manager must have access to resources such as money and facilities. Second, a manager must establish lines of information in order to stay "in the know" both formally and informally. Last, a manager must have the support or backing of others in the organization to accomplish his or her job.

Kanter warns, "People at the top need to insulate themselves from the routine operations of the organization in order to develop and exercise power. But this very insulation can lead to another source of powerlessness—lack of information."[6]

Economist John Kenneth Galbraith defines power as "the relative ability to influence group decisions."[7] He then goes on to explain the importance of experience in acquiring power. "Experience within the higher levels of a corporation provides access to all sorts of arcane knowledge: marketing knowledge, legal knowledge, or even how to find one's way through and around the Washington bureaucracy. All these forms of knowledge provide opportunities for greater power."[8]

INFORMATION OVERLOAD

Information overload is one of the most serious handicaps facing today's business manager and government executive. In the Industrial Society the critical problems were the lack of information and the inability to retrieve it. Now, with access to so much information, the ability to make decisions and resolve conflicts is limited simply because so much time is spent going over all the pertinent and peripheral information bearing on every subject within the area of operation.

Aleksander I. Solzhenitsyn commented on information overload in his commencement address at Harvard University on June 8, 1978. He stated, "In spite of the abundance of information, or maybe partly because of it, the West has great difficulty in finding its bearings amid contemporary events."[9]

Within the last 20 years, three-fourths of all the information available to the world has been developed. Information doubles every 10 years. According to a Xerox advertisement, each year 72 billion pieces of new information are disseminated. These statistics provide overwhelming evidence that the information overload problem is valid and critical.

The manager in the information-intensive enterprise or government agency must determine what information he or she needs to know in order to act. Since information has a price tag, the cost of collecting all information on a specific subject must be carefully scrutinized. Nice-to-know information is not only costly, but may actually hinder the decision-making process. Need to know must be the primary guideline for effective managers. The economic doctrine of E. F. Schumacher, summarized in the title of his book, *Small Is Beautiful: Economics As If People Mattered* (New York: Harper & Row, 1975), is most relevant to resolving the problem of information overload.

There is another aspect to excess information which impoverishes rather than enriches the enterprise. This is the endless grinding out of seemingly needless and redundant information to others, much of it demanded by federal regulations. A study conducted in 1978 by the Office of Management and Budget shows that Americans spend 785 million hours a year filling out 4,987 various federal forms. Industry spends $24 to $32 billion annually to meet federal information requirements. So the costs of overloading the information system must be considered and all ways to lower these costs must be explored.

Within organizations, the compulsion to write memos and reports for personal public relations rather than for dissemination of helpful information ties up the time of the people who prepare these self-serving documents as well as the time of all those who receive and read useless "puffery" information.

The managers who "demerchandise" information and perform their tasks with the best and least—not necessarily the most—information will ultimately gain and maintain power. The proper use of information is the hallmark of a successful manager.

INFORMATION AND MOTIVATION

As a manager, you manage not only physical resources, but also human resources—people are your stock in trade. To manage people you must first understand what motivates them. Although the motivating factors of the Industrial Age are still operating in the Age of Information, their emphasis has shifted and they need to be expanded and augmented.

Underlying the theory of motivation is the concept of individual needs. Needs create drives, and drives, in turn, make people act or react to achieve a goal. "Need satisfaction" occurs when the goal is reached. When the need is fulfilled it is no longer a motivating factor for the individual, and the person seeks out fulfillment of other needs.

The psychologist Abraham H. Maslow categorized human needs into five basic levels and ranked them in a hierarchy of importance, from fundamental physiological needs to intellectual needs of self-fulfillment. His criterion was that needs in the lower levels must be fairly well satisfied before needs in the upper levels begin to motivate a person.

Maslow's five levels of needs are as follows. Physiological needs are the needs for food, clothing, and shelter; these are the basic needs one must satisfy to survive. Safety and security needs make up the next level. People want to maintain and protect what they have acquired. At this level, a person is motivated to put money away for future use. When the individual has accomplished a feeling of stability, he is at the middle level of the hierarchy. Social needs are now of primary importance. These needs are characterized by a feeling of wanting to belong to groups and the desire to share and associate—wanting to be loved. Ego needs, which are at the fourth level, are twofold. First, they relate to self-esteem, that is, a person's feeling of self-confidence, achievement, competence, and knowledge. Second, ego needs are fulfilled by others when a person achieves a reputation for excellence. This involves the respect a person earns from his peer group, the status, recognition, and appreciation he achieves. At the pinnacle of the hierarchy of needs, Maslow placed self-fulfillment needs: the needs for personal and professional growth. They encompass the concept of self-actualization—the accomplishment of fulfilling one's own potential as a human being.

In the Age of Information, there are proportionately fewer people in the poverty class in developed countries and so survival and safety needs no longer predominate. Even social needs are fairly well satisfied by most people. The upward shift in the hierarchy to levels four and five becomes the main focus of attention. With an emphasis on formal education and training and the emergence of the expert, managers must now try to fulfill the ego and self-actualization needs of their employees.

This echoes the research of Frederick Herzberg in the most requested reprint from *Harvard Business Review,* "One More Time: How Do You Motivate Employees?" According to Herzberg, "The growth or *motivator* factors that are intrinsic to the job are: achievement, recognition for achievement, the work itself, and growth or advancement."[10]

And when economist John Kenneth Galbraith was asked what the primary motivation for managers is, he replied, "There's no question that the corporation succeeds because of the motivation associated with peer approval. People working together in the corporation—or in the government or in a university, for that matter—are motivated overwhelmingly by their desire to have the good opinion of their colleagues. Without this, the modern corporation would be a failure. Now the second most important motivation is the direct reward of growth."[11]

Today an additional need must be recognized: the need to know. At the University of California (Berkeley), a study of job satisfaction items was designed to measure Maslow's needs categories. The investigators analyzed the responses of 380 managers from six organizations. They found ". . . that the 'need-to-know' exists separately from other needs in the Maslow hierarchy and might be a unique dimension of job satisfaction or dissatisfaction."[12]

Fulfilling an individual's need to know in an organization is an important function of management. Not only do subordinates and peers need to have the feeling of being informed, but your supervisors must also feel that they are in the know about current and future events. When you consult people on decisions you arouse in them a feeling of having inside information on what is happening. Although the need to know exists at all levels of Maslow's hierarchy of needs, the demands of the new society mandate that it take precedence over all other needs.

There is a mistaken belief that since people in both management and nonmanagement positions are preoccupied with realizing their ego and self-fulfillment needs, money is no longer a great motivator. Money is still a primary driving force for motivating people. Moreover, it appears not only in weekly paychecks, but in the form of employee benefits and management perquisites, usually referred to as "perks." Some of the more common employee benefits that translate into actual dollars are health insurance, life insurance, long-term disability plans, pension plans, and performance sharing plans. The IRS has ruled that many management perks are the same as money and are thus taxable as personal income; perks in this category include use of company cars and limousines and company-paid country club dues when the car or club are for personal use. But many perks are tax-free.

Money talks. Money itself is a status symbol and represents authority and power. Even in the international arena we talk of dollar diplomacy. Edward J. Piszek, millionaire owner of the fishcake factory known as Mrs. Paul's Kitchens, understands the authority the dollar bill affords. He has rephrased the Golden Rule to read: "The guy with the gold makes the rules."[13] Multimillionaire Joseph R. McMicking, the original financial backer of Ampex Corp., also practices the Golden Rule. As he has said, "I live by the golden rule. I've got the gold. I make the rules."[14] Make no mistake, money does make the difference. If you have two jobs and are rich, you have diversified interests. If you have two jobs and are poor, you're moonlighting.

A "Special Consumer Survey" by The Conference Board in July 1978 disclosed that the older workers get and the more money they earn the more satisfied they are with their jobs. The study further indicated that 87 percent of Americans are satisfied or very satisfied with their work. A 1980 Louis Harris & Associates survey of white collar workers revealed that office workers felt increased salaries was the most motivating factor to improve productivity.

The big reason people work is to earn a living. Money not only motivates people to fulfill their basic needs, but is used to accomplish the other things a person wants from life. But most employees and many managers do not know what they are receiving in the way of benefits. Drs. Richard C. Huseman and John D. Hatfield of the Department of Management at the University of Georgia constructed a model in which they listed the seven underlying motives for instituting a benefits program: (1) attract good employees, (2) reduce turnover, (3) motivate employees, (4) increase job satisfaction, (5) improve employee morale, (6) keep the union out, and (7) enhance the organization's image among employees. But according to the authors, "Obviously, employees lack substantive, accurate knowledge of their benefits. Because they are unaware of the benefit package, it is understandable that attaining benefit program goals is severely impeded."[15] This illustrates the importance of the "need to inform" as a major force in motivating people to improve their performance and productivity.

INFORMATION AND PRODUCTIVITY

In the Age of Information, productivity attains a new dimension—the production of knowledge as well as goods and services. As Peter F. Drucker has written, "There are factors of substantial if not decisive impact on productivity that never become visible cost figures. First there is knowledge—man's most productive resource if properly applied, but also the most expensive one, and totally unproductive, if misapplied."[16]

The term productivity has a bad reputation, particularly among nonmanagement personnel. Many workers equate the word with speed, and think that increasing productivity entails working faster and harder for the same remuneration. Such is not the case. Productivity is more than production output over labor input. The inputs of information, equipment, energy, and materials must also be included. The effective manager will be able to increase productivity of an organization, not by working harder and longer, but by working smarter and more efficiently—by knowing where information is, how to get at it promptly, and how to put it to work most effectively.

In a *U.S. News & World Report* interview with C. Jackson Grayson, Jr., chairman of the American Productivity Center, the following question and answer helped to clarify the much used word "productivity."

Q: "Productivity" is a word that causes a lot of confusion. How do you define it?

A: It is a measure of the efficiency with which people produce goods and services. The simplest definition is that it's the ratio between what you get out for what you put in.

Too often, productivity is mistakenly associated with layoffs, stopwatches, and a speedup on the assembly line. That's the wrong impression. To measure productivity, we have to include not only the man-hours that go into a job but also the capital, the machinery and tools, the input of energy and raw materials.[17]

You improve the productivity of your employees by job enhancement, not by job enlargement. You need to draw on the information people already possess (which takes special skills on your part), and then use that information for innovative, productive methods. At Texas Instruments in Dallas, semiconductor assemblers informed management that a lot of time could be saved if their spools of wire held more wire. When bigger spools were used, the time spent changing spools was cut in half. Other such innovations at Texas Instruments have increased the company's productivity 15 percent a year for the last 10 years.

In the Industrial Age the main thrust was on worker productivity. Today, the emphasis has shifted to management productivity. A manager's productivity is based on his or her handling of information to improve individual or organizational outputs. Job obsolescence occurs about every seven years in this information-intensive society unless individuals participate in continuing education programs or adopt other methods of keeping up with new ideas and breakthroughs. A different breed of people are engaged in business, industry, and government—people who are self-motivated to achieve personal and group goals. Management must provide these knowledge workers with the information they need to keep themselves current in their particular fields. The payoff to management is a cadre of highly productive workers who provide the organization with new products and services and the competitive edge that results in profits.

Measuring information productivity must be addressed in a new setting. Numbers of reports produced, job turnaround time, and statistical summaries of printouts are not meaningful enough in this era. Productivity must be measured in terms of how valuable the information is to the organization and how efficiently the information is provided to the user. User satisfaction becomes a prime element in the information-oriented organization.

Accuracy of information is another major criterion of evaluation. Acting on inaccurate information at the start of a program may defeat the end objectives. If the error is discovered too late for the investment in capital and labor to be recovered, the program is doomed.

Adequacy of information is still another element to be judged. Even if the information may be accurate, is there enough information to make a decision with some degree of confidence? Or is there an overabundance of information—so much that the critical items that are needed cannot be separated from the surplus data? Reliability of information must be measured also. Does the information hold up under repeated tests, or is it only a momentary phenomenon that cannot be relied upon for significant problem solving? Timeliness of information is another criterion to be considered in measuring information productivity. Is the information the latest and the best and has it been delivered in time to be useful?

A final measure of productivity is accessibility of the information. Can the ultimate user gain access to the information directly or will a series of routines and procedures cause delays and frustrations?

These are the criteria that the manager must use in cutting costs of and increasing payoffs from information. The new manager must be aware of the critical importance of information within the organization and must know how to use that information most profitably. Information does affect productivity. Therefore, it must be used economically and skillfully just as any other valuable resource is used.

THE POWER OF NEGATIVE INFORMATION

Theoretically, information should be completely objective: free of emotion. Actually, information is fraught with feelings. Providing information that is positive and reinforces what the boss wants to hear is never a problem. Difficulties start when one has to offer news that is negative and unwanted and that disagrees with preconceived ideas.

As John and Mark Arnold reported in *The Wall Street Journal,* "For fear of being labeled negative or disloyal, managers in many companies practice a kind of benign deception, refusing to honestly voice their concerns or call attention to problems, mistakes, and misjudgments in time to be easily corrected."[18]

Classical literature and music, from Roman and Greek epics to Chinese operas, are filled with stories of bearers of bad news who are beheaded for delivering accurate (but unpleasant) information. Legends are filled with stories of messengers who, because they fear fatal reprisal for disturbing the peace of mind of their emperors, delay delivery of vital information until it is too late to take positive action, thus causing the empire to collapse. The ruler considers the bad-news bearer to be the cause of the negative information and orders the messenger slain.

Adolph Hitler was inclined to listen only to what he wanted to believe. In the summer of 1940 the German intelligence people got possession of a report accurately projecting America's aircraft production. According to Ladislas Farago, in his book, *The Game of the Foxes,*

> The report stirred the Abwehr to instant activity. Admiral Canaris, not yet intimidated by Hitler's scornful rejection of intelligence reports that did not bear out his own calculations or confirm his intuition, personally handled this particular project. He took the paper to Hitler. It was of no use. The Fuhrer shrugged it off, and even threatened to punish those who believed or circulated such "defeatist rubbish."[19]

Unfortunately, this behead-the-messenger syndrome still exists in corporate boardrooms and government organizations.

Regardless of how well documented the facts were, Hitler was never convinced that he was wrong. Even with the Russians only a few kilometers from Berlin, Hitler dismissed intelligence reports that were unfavorable to the German position, scribbling on their covers, "This cannot be."

In the Age of Information the ability to provide needed, but sometimes negative, information is vital. The manager who finds ways to deliver bad news and still survive eventually becomes a major force in the organization. One of the best ways to soften the blow of negative information is to precede the unwelcome news with some positive statement. This "buffer effect" at least arouses and holds the attention of the listener until the unpleasant message can be delivered. The psychological order of presentation of good news before bad news prevents the ego-defensiveness that bad news engenders. Then offer several alternative courses of action that the executive may take to recoup position or minimize loss. The alternatives may be offered in preferential order, with the final decision made by the superior.

Another way of presenting disturbing information is to have it issued by a third party, such as a consultant to the organization or a member of the firm who is not directly involved with the subject. Of course, this may jeopardize the message bearer's position, and the person who instigates delivery of the message gets no credit for preventing a bad decision based on the unpleasant news. Similarly, submitting the information anonymously may aid the organization, but again, the instigator receives no recognition or reward for his alertness. The credibility of an anonymous letter is low.

Many of you may be in the position of receiving rather than dispensing unwanted news. In such a case, set up a channel by which negative information can be transmitted to you without fear of retaliation. Encourage subordinates to reveal when things are going poorly. Develop a willingness to listen to other points of view, and indicate by your own actions that you welcome all ideas—even those in conflict with your own.

In a *U.S. News & World Report* interview with James L. Hayes, president of the American Management Associations, the following question and answer focused on the importance of listening.

Q: Mr. Hayes, managers are always looking for ways to get more production from employees. How can a boss motivate workers to do a better job?

A: I think company managements overstress the whole idea of worker motivation. Basically, people motivate themselves. The task of the boss is to create a climate for job satisfaction.

There's no reason why a person shouldn't be as comfortable doing his job as he is when he's not working. If he's unhappy, there's generally something wrong at the management level.

Perhaps the No. 1 fault with American management is that executives, even in the biggest corporations, don't get out of their offices and listen to what workers have to say.

Listening, being alert to problems is part of the art of supervision. Most small companies have this ease of communication between worker and boss. Big companies are hurting themselves when they don't encourage their supervisors to practice it.[20]

REFERENCES

1. Harvey L. Poppel, "The Information Revolution: Winners and Losers," *Harvard Business Review,* January–February 1978, p. 159.
2. Eric Norden, "Playboy Interview: Saul Alinsky," *Playboy,* March 1972, p. 62.
3. John Dean's testimony at hearings before the Select Committee on Presidential Campaign Activities of the United States Senate, 93rd Congress, 1st Session (Presidential Campaign Activities of 1972, Senate Resolution 60), Watergate and Related Activities, Phase I: Watergate Investigation, Washington, D.C., June 25 and 26, 1973, Book 3, pp. 1,017–1,018.
4. William O. Douglas, *Points of Rebellion* (New York: Random House, 1970), p. 32.
5. "Machines That Think," *Newsweek,* June 30, 1980, p. 51. Copyright 1980, by Newsweek, Inc. All Rights Reserved. Reprinted by Permission.
6. Rosabeth Moss Kanter, "Power Failure in Management Circuits," *Harvard Business Review,* July–August 1979, p. 71.
7. Zack Russ, "An Interview with John Kenneth Galbraith . . . Inflation, the Economy, and Executive Power," *Management Review,* July 1978, p. 16.
8. *Ibid,* p. 16.
9. Aleksander Solzhenitsyn, A World Split Apart (New York: Harper & Row, 1978), p. 39.
10. Frederick Herzberg, "One More Time: How Do You Motivate Employees?" *Harvard Business Review,* January–February 1968, p. 57.
11. Russ, *op. cit.,* p. 15.
12. Karlene H. Roberts, Gordon A. Walter, and Raymond E. Miles, "A Factor Analytic Study of Job Satisfaction Items Designed to Measure Maslow Need Categories," *Personnel Psychology,* 24:2 (1971), p. 219.
13. "One-man Crusade Against the Polish Joke," *Life,* January 14, 1972, p. 70. © 1972 Time, Inc. All Rights Reserved. Reprinted by Permission.
14. "The Golden Ruler," *Newsweek,* January 10, 1972, p. 55. Copyright 1972, by Newsweek, Inc. All Rights Reserved. Reprinted by Permission.
15. Richard C. Huseman and John D. Hatfield, "Communicating Employee Benefits: Directions for Future Research," *The Journal of Busi-*

ness Communication, 15: 4 (Summer 1978), p. 4. By permission from The American Business Communication Association, 911 South Sixth Street, University of Illinois, Champaign, IL 61820, publishers of *The Journal of Business Communication.*

16. Peter F. Drucker, *Management: Tasks, Responsibilities, Practices* (New York: Harper & Row, 1974), p. 70.

17. "Why U.S. Workers Are Producing Less," *U.S. News & World Report,* May 1, 1978, p. 95. © 1978.

18. John Arnold and Mark Arnold, "Corporate Coverups," *The Wall Street Journal,* June 5, 1978, col. 3, p. 18. Reprinted by permission of *The Wall Street Journal,* © Dow Jones & Company, Inc. 1978. All rights reserved.

19. Ladislas Farago, *The Game of the Foxes* (New York: McKay, 1971), p.409.

20. "Want to Be a Better Boss? Advice from an Expert," *U.S. News & World Report,* March 21, 1977, p. 68. © 1977.

3

INFORMATION TECHNOLOGY—
A MANAGEMENT TOOL

No single development will have a greater impact on U.S. business in the next decade than the technologies associated with information processing. They are radically changing the way in which products are designed and manufactured, in which managements organize and run companies, and in which companies communicate and do business with one another.[1]

—*R. B. Alexander*

Voluminous data exist on the technologies associated with the Age of Information, but there is little coverage of how managers can use these tools to improve themselves, their performance, their organizations, and society as a whole.

The concurrent development, convergence, and merger of computers and communications technologies were the driving forces that evolved into the Age of Information. They continue to give impetus to today's information-intensive society.

COMMUNICATIONS TECHNOLOGY

Communications technology can be traced to prehistoric cave drawings in Europe. But the communications technology that is generally associated with business and government organizations is linked with the typewriter, which made its appearance in the eighteenth century. This country was still in the pre-industrial era when the telephone was invented. In 1876 the United States Patent Office issued Patent Number 174465 to Alexander Graham Bell for "The method of and apparatus for transmitting vocal or other sounds telegraphically. . . ." More than a century later society still feels the impact of these two ubiquitous machines.

But it is not the ever-increasing use of the typewriter, telephone, and other office equipment that is as important as how you as manager or administrator use this equipment for more effective and efficient operations.

The single major element common to all communications technologies is the individual. The primary purpose for the development of communication techniques is improving communications among human beings. Yet, too often the blinking lights and glaring video display terminals of the "office of the future" blind today's managers to the fact that the office is made up of people, and that these people are interdependent and must coordinate their activities through *communication*. The passé McLuhan thesis that the medium is the message does not hold up in the business and government organization. The medium may influence the impact of the message, but it is not the message.

Managers in the Age of Information can use electronic communication tools to turn their offices into profit centers for their organizations. But one major barrier must be overcome: resistance to change, which is a bifurcated problem. First, there is fear of change from the people who work with you and who will be handling the new equipment. Their fear is based on a perceived threat of job loss due to automation or their own inability to cope with new machinery. By bringing the office staff into the planning stages of the modernization of your office you will do much to alleviate this problem. Whenever possible, get the opinions of your staff as to which model typewriter, copying machine, or microform viewer they would prefer using. By encouraging their participation in the decision-making level of the paperless office you give them the feeling that management cares about their opinions.

Second, many managers themselves fear the onset of the electronic office. They are unfamiliar with the new equipment and realize that the way they operated their offices in the past is not practical in the office of today. For example, one of the biggest hurdles to overcome in installing a word processing system within a company is the resistance by managers who have come to the appalling realization that they will be losing their secretaries in the new office organization. Another example of management resistance comes with the introduction of on-line terminals into the manager's offices. Many managers think that using a keyboard to communicate with a computer—which is similar to typing on a typewriter—is a low-level task, and for this reason refuse to participate in the "demeaning" system. Attitudes must change before the benefits from communications technology are realized.

INFORMATION-ORIENTED OFFICES

To perform your role as a manager in business, industry, or government, you must be familiar with the most effective tools you can use to do your job. To best understand the technologies that are available to you, look at the information-oriented office from three aspects: generating information, processing information, and disseminating information. Some equipment may overlap these three functions.

Information may be generated in oral, written, or graphic form. For years the standard oral form was by dictating to a secretary who took information in shorthand and transcribed it into a typewritten format. Today's mobile manager may want to generate information at home, on a plane, or in an automobile, where no secretary is available. The solution: dictation equipment.

Regardless of the dictation equipment used, the problem lies, not in the hardware, but in getting managers to organize their thoughts in a manner that is clearly understood by the listener (and eventual reader). Most managers prefer to use written information for transcription, because they don't know how to prepare oral messages. The competitive edge goes to the office where dictation is the main mode of entering information into the system. Managers who effectively dictate their messages on tapes or belts are six times as efficient as people who have handwritten drafts typed.

Information Processing
Information processing is where it's happening—where the activity takes place. In 1969 IBM introduced the Magnetic Tape Selec-

tric Typewriter (MT/ST), coined the term "word processing," and heralded the arrival of the electronic office. Only a few years ago, a typist prepared your data; the output was sheaves of paper. Now, once your information is given to a secretary or a word processing center, your input is typed on a keyboard and captured in electronic form.

Typewriters with brains can store frequently used phrases, erase errors without backspacing, and align columns of figures. These smart machines transmit messages via telephone lines to other clever typewriters within the same company or across the nation.

With the evolution of the paperless office, you, the manager, begin to work with information itself rather than with the information media. You can recall information from different sources on a video screen, retain all information pertinent to your current needs, store the unused portions, and synthesize the resulting information into new concepts and new markets. Your importance to your organization will be in direct proportion to your ability to manipulate information. Word processing is not limited to correspondence and reports. The entry, editing, storing, retrieving, and transmitting functions will be used for problem solving, decision making, and business forecasting. With information in an electronic medium you are no longer a paper shuffler—you're an information user in a paperless office.

The Telephone

Information dissemination is closely associated with the telephone. However, alert managers realize that this office standby encompasses functions of information generation and processing as well. In an environment where information is paramount, the telephone is the management tool that saves time and effort, makes your money work harder, increases sales, and produces good customer service.

With the cost of letters soaring, mail delivery lagging, and the cost of an average industrial sales call edging past $80, the typical $5 telephone sales call is a bargain for the budget-conscious competitive business person. The Bell System's Phone-Power program emphasizes how you can use your telephone to introduce new products, open new accounts, sell on service calls, keep customers buying from you, collect overdue accounts, revive inactive accounts, and reply to letters. And remember, the key element is not new technology but the human factor in using the telephone as a management tool.

For example, consider an eight-step phone call for opening new accounts. First, identify yourself and your company in a direct manner and use your prospect's name. Second, show your prospect that you know something about him and his business and thus establish rapport. Next, comment on an interest-creating situation such as, "With your anniversay sale coming up, I'm sure you'd be able to use our new product to stimulate sales." Fourth, ask questions that will give you more insight into the prospect's business so you can tailor your sales message to his needs. Fifth, deliver your sales message in a positive mode that emphasizes benefits over features. Sixth, resolve any objections your customer might have about your product or service. Then close the sale with a forced-choice question such as, "Which model do you want us to send you?" Eight is the wrap-up in which you confirm the order, arrange for a call-back, and offer a sincere thank you for the new order. In spite of attempts to automate information, it is still a human activity.

Although sophisticated telephone systems and computerized communication networks speed up information delivery and extend its coverage, the name of the game is people. If people are conspicuously absent, the result can be unsatisfactory. The automatic answering and recording service is a case in point. The personalized contact that is lost by the prerecorded message can, in some cases, result in a loss of customers that is more expensive than any cost savings the gadget was expected to yield. Here's why: When you make a phone call you presume that another person will answer the telephone and listen to what you have to say. Thus, when your anticipations are not fulfilled you become temporarily disoriented. The disorientation may even last so long that you miss the prerecorded message and become even more frustrated in your attempts to communicate.

To overcome this impersonal approach to communication, some phone systems allow callers who feel the need to talk to another person to do so after the message has been played. The reassurance that comes from contact with a live human being on the other end of the line calms the caller, although such contact may not add information to the taped message.

Certain prerecorded messages, such as time and temperature recordings, do not require personalized contact. Also, if all you want to communicate is your statement on a particular issue or specific data such as a new telephone number, no feedback is required and no human being is needed.

If you want to know what your congressmen are doing on Capitol Hill, you can dial a three-minute taped summary of the current happenings in Congress. The Chamber of Commerce of the United States provides this in a capsule comment called Washington Dial. And there's hardly a city that does not offer a Dial-A-Prayer number. Whether the message you phone for is political or spiritual, it is impersonal in that *your* reactions are unrecorded.

The Dial-A-Number epidemic that is sweeping America is going commercial. The phone companies have teamed with the National Weather Service to provide a Dial-A-Forecast system. Sponsors advertise their product prior to issuing the weather forecast. A similar service is Sports Phone, in New York, which provides each caller with a one-minute scoreboard—preceded by a seven-second commercial. The New York Telephone Company provides Dial-A-Joke, and this averages about 50,000 calls daily. A radio station in Pittsfield, Massachusetts—WBEC—offers Dial-A-Laugh. When the special number is dialed the listener is treated to a 25-second recording of a staff member laughing. This is surely the ultimate service in impersonal dialed messages.

Consumerism encourages large businesses to use the phone lines in another role. Customers are urged to vent their complaints to toll-free numbers on an 800-line. Ralph Nader has said of these phone lines in general, "The returns aren't in yet, but it's easier to set up toll-free telephone lines so consumers can rid themselves of their anger then it is to improve the product which caused the problem."[2] As an example of what Nader refers to, the Bureau of Mines installed a "hot line" by which coal miners could report safety violations, anonymously, if they wished. The caller dialed a number in the office of the deputy director of the Bureau of Mines. A prerecorded instruction was given the caller who then recorded his complaint. According to the bureau, a top bureau official was supposed to act on the information on the next working day. However, the bureau admitted it had not checked the tape recorded calls for two months and had even failed to service the device when it went out of order!

Motorola Corporation uses the telephone "hot line" concept in reverse. It strongly urges its distributor to call "Quasar" television buyers within three months of purchase to ask if there are any problems. The cliche, "Don't call us, we'll call you," has now acquired a new meaning in the Age of Information. As Byron Nichols, Vice President for Consumer Affairs at Chrysler, explains, "A corporation is, by definition, an artificial person, sort of a faceless thing. If you give people someone to call, then you've taken a big step toward eradicating that faceless thing." The human element is a basic ingredient of communication. When automation enhances the personal aspect of communication there is a positive contribution. When the mechanistic elements depersonalize the communication the results are frustration, confusion, and havoc.

The telephone is often used as a status symbol. The unlisted phone number is one phenomenon in the use of the telephone for prestige purposes. Although many subscribers request unlisted numbers to avoid obscene phone calls, harassing messages, and phone solicitations, many people delist themselves solely for purposes of self-esteem. Telephone companies have tried unsuccessfully to discourage unlisted phone numbers and even charge a monthly fee for this "privilege." In large cities such as New York, Chicago, and Washington, D.C., more than 20 percent of the subscribers are unlisted. In California—a state studded with movie stars—not one movie star's phone number appears in a public telephone directory. For those who want to use the phone companies to suggest their social station the rule seems to be: If you want to gain prestige, don't publish your telephone number.

Telephone status within an organization is epitomized by this episode involving senate majority and minority leaders. When Majority Leader Lyndon B. Johnson had a telephone installed in his limousine, Republican Minority Leader Everett Dirksen promptly retaliated by having a phone installed in *his* official government car. But status is meaningless unless it is recognized—so the senator from Illinois placed a limousine-to-limousine call to LBJ. Senator Dirksen was put down in true Texas style when LBJ interrupted their conversation, saying, "Just a minute, Ev, I've got a call on my other phone."

Facsimile and Electronic Meetings

Tied in with the telephone is the electronic mailbox, also known as facsimile. Facsimile is the telecommunication of graphic images—such as drawings, photographs, or typed pages—via the public telephone system. The process was invented in 1842, but was not put to practical use until newspaper wirephoto services were introduced in the 1920s. Renewed interest in facsimile in the office is the result of increased speed of transmission, reliability, and ease of operation; high image quality; improved paper; and advances in equipment compatibility. It used to take four to six minutes to transmit an 8½" x 11" document; now, new systems have cut the time to less than a minute.

Inexpensive electronic mail transmission will soon be a common management tool. Fast and cost-effective facsimile systems are now available to organizations so that time-sensitive graphic information may be transmitted over telephone lines in seconds. Speed is increased and errors are reduced. Words and figures that could be misunderstood if described over the telephone can be accurately transmitted.

The equipment may be leased or you may use the facilities of commercial electronic mail transmission services located throughout the United States. A directory of U.S. electronic mail drops lists 150 locations in 111 cities and 42 states.[3]

Teleconferencing is now a practical reality and electronic meetings are commonplace. With the emergence of conglomerates and multinational corporations, teleconferencing has become a necessity to overcome the problem of space and time. Even more importantly, it permits managers to increase their span of control.

Video teleconferencing is best exemplified by the AT&T picturephone. Picturephone Meeting Service is available in this country between any two of these five cities: New York, San Francisco, Los Angeles, Chicago, and Washington, D.C. An hour-long coast-to-coast meeting costs $400—that's less than the round-trip plane fare for just one person from New York to San Francisco. The meeting rooms are each equipped with three automatic cameras, which will photograph displays of new designs, complex formulas, and any other visual aids. There are two viewing screens in each room; one for receiving the incoming picture and one for monitoring your own presentation. You can even videotape the picturephone meeting and store it for future reference.

However, automated information transmission does have drawbacks. The much-heralded picturephone can offer too much togetherness as far as some Americans are concerned. The 10 videophones installed at 1600 Pennsylvania Avenue were removed after the free-of-charge experimental period ended. The official reason given for hanging up the TV phone was that the budget officers could not justify the expense. But some Washington wags speculated that the users felt as if Big Brother were watching them.

Computer teleconferencing allows more flexibility than video teleconferencing does. Conference participants type their messages on a computer terminal and the message is printed on all the terminals in the computer network. Participants can look at the printouts at their convenience and respond to ideas after verifying data or consulting with other individuals. The main shortcoming in the system is that there is no face-to-face contact.

The conference call is another type of electronic meeting: the audio teleconference. Although more limited than video or computer teleconferencing, audio teleconferencing can be enhanced by using facsimile equipment to transmit graphic information.

Computer Technology

The technological phenomenon of the computer's evolution has been well documented. But the computer's impact on business and government management practices has had little publicity, despite the very real impact that computer technology has had in these two areas.

The computer is a powerful management tool that, during the last decade, has become faster, smaller, cheaper, and smarter. The qualitative side of this quantitative analysis of computers deserves attention. The software (or programs) used in the computer have become more sophisticated. All members of the organization can use a computer that has preprogrammed functions. People without technical training can handle material that previously would have required the use of complex mathematics and logic.

You can use the computer effectively to conduct the management process and decision-making activities of your organization. Upper-echelon managers have a tendency to concentrate on the technical aspects of electronic or computerized systems, and to neglect their ultimate uses as tools for you, the manager or administrator.

The management process is a six-fold sequence in which decisions must be made at each level. The computer can be invaluable at each step. First, at the conceptual stage, is goal-setting. You must identify what you want to achieve. What are your objectives? What are your goals? What is your purpose? In the business world and in the real-politik of government, you do everything with a purpose in mind. In this step you can use your computer to list your goals and establish your priorities in the context of the charter of your organization. You can evaluate their effects on other organizational goals, determine the feasibility of achieving your goals within the existing economic, social, and political environments, and measure them in monetary and social benefits. These multifactor considerations can be manipulated quickly and completely on a computer to select those goals that will best benefit your organization and you.

The planning function is the second element of the management process. At this stage, you must expand the conceptual ideas embedded in goal-setting. You can use the computer to determine reasonable time frames, set basic standards, provide detailed specifications, and identify sub-goals that will led you to your ultimate objectives. Assuredly, this could be done manually, but a computer can handle these various elements more efficiently, pinpoint those elements that conflict, and highlight areas where more information is needed.

Programming is the third phase of the management process in which you as a manager may use the computer to come up with specific operations that will build upon each other to achieve your ultimate goals. The computer can list an array of activities that you may employ to reach your goals and then weight each activity according to its contribution to the overall goals. Incompatible elements are eliminated, and the remainder are scheduled for overall objectives.

Budgeting, the fourth factor, is a management decision that tells your organization you are putting your money where your mouth is. Of course, budgeting encompasses more than money: It involves allocating labor, facilities, and your personal energies to attain the overall goals. In essence, it is your commitment to the ultimate purpose. Computers were first used in finance operations and they are still powerful tools for allocating dollars, deploying human resources, and determining available facilities to accomplish your ideas. The computer can aid you in determining how much money to commit to your ultimate goal, can keep track of how well you are staying within budget limitations, can signal you when expenditures are exceeding or underrunning commitments, and can help you analyze ways to reestablish financial priorities if unexpected events affect your goals.

Implementing your programs to meet plans and eventual goals constitutes the fifth segment in the management process. Again, you can use information fed into your computer to monitor the programs, not only from a budgetary point of view, but also from the standpoint of how well these programs are fulfilling your expectations. This operational information keeps you abreast of what you are doing incrementally to achieve your initial ideas.

The final element in your management process is evaluat. ,n. Feedback begins the management process all over again, for it alerts you to the necessary adjustments and changes you must make to reach your objectives. Here again, you will use your computer as a management tool to evaluate how effective you have been in achieving your initial plans.

The management process begins, ends, and begins again with information. You do not have to understand bits, bytes, and bauds to hire a computer to work effectively for you. What you do need to know is that you can and will use computer technology to process raw data into information for your needs.

As a manager, be aware that all of these advancements in computers and other technological equipment should be considered only as interrelated tools; they are not automated management. Managers are coming to realize that they must use all the tools technology has to offer. Word processing provides documentation and data processing manipulates, stores, and retrieves information; in many companies, these two systems are being combined to further facilitate management decision making.

INTEGRATED INFORMATION SYSTEMS

The information manager must integrate the technological driving forces that impact the management of private and public sector organizations. This does not imply the necessity for a total information system, but rather the need for a focal point for providing managers with the best tools to acquire, evaluate, and use information for maximum potential.

New concepts in facilities planning for information services are a necessity. The static, fixed-site ideas must be expanded to include the dynamic, flexible, on-line remote terminals that pervade the information economy.

Fixed Site

The initial phase should start with the establishment of a single site. The selection of the site will be determined by its convenience to the ultimate users—the management elements of your organization. Your fixed-site communication system can be set up in one of two locations. If a technical information center or special library already exists in your organization, it probably contains special equipment for maintaining and using the information stored in it. The second facility to consider is the corporate "war room" or briefing center, where managers monitor and control the operation of their organization. This room contains all of the facilities for visually displaying current progress and simulating potential business scenarios. The room may evolve from a simple chart room into an area that provides rear screen projectors, video display screens, and multimedia devices. If much of the information to be used in the corporate war room is to be maintained in the special library, then the two facilities should adjoin each other. However, with the telecommunications hardware now available, the information center can be linked directly with the "war room."

On-Line Terminal Rooms

When you are ready to install on-line terminal rooms, be sure to allocate at least 100 square feet to allow room for an information specialist and two users. To avoid transmission interference, the electrical outlets used for the terminal must be restricted to terminal usage and a specific telephone extension must be exclusively reserved for the remote terminal. The information specialist must be able to dial directly into a Tymnet or Tymshare facility without going through a switchboard, where inadvertent disconnections and delays are possible.

Determining the proper terminal can be confusing if you do not have appropriate criteria for making your decisions. Do you need a print terminal or cathode-ray-tube (CRT) display screen with a printer attachment? Evaluate the merits and costs of low- *vs.* high-speed access. (The speed of access is a characteristic that affects the cost of searching. Higher speeds require less computer time.) Portable *vs.* stationary units is a third criterion to be assessed. Regarding transportability, you must consider size, weight, carrying case, and telephone coupler. The lease or buy evaluation must also be made, as well as decisions on maintenance and service. Printing supplies can have a significant effect on the operating costs and must also be considered in the total evaluation. Other elements such as operating noise levels, ease of operation, and print or display clarity must also be assessed.

The furniture should include a table long enough to hold a terminal, printer, and cassette tape deck. In addition, there should be a bookcase to store manuals and searching tools needed for the various data bases. If some of the searching tools are in microform, a microfiche reader is also needed.

THE MOUNTAIN AND THE MANAGER

Francis Bacon wrote the much quoted adage, "If the mountain will not come to Mahomet, Mahomet must go to the mountain." Unlike Mahomet, today's manager does not have to go to the mountain of information; it can come to him directly or through an intermediary, the information specialist. For example, if a manager telephones the organization's information center with a question, the information staff can locate the answer and then display it on a CRT terminal located in the inquiring director's office.

The fast-tracker in business, industry, and government has replaced his attaché case with a portable terminal for on-line searching from home or hotel room. Thus, the mobile manager may access mountains of information from wherever he may be. Many a congressman travels among his constituency accompanied by his portable terminal. These lawmakers can dial a data base in Washington, D.C., that prints out lists of programs that can be tapped to aid their importunate local residents.

An information specialist with a remote terminal should attend all important conferences. The specialist can tap the various data bases for information pertaining to the conference subjects as they are discussed.

On-line graphic display systems are now available to display business trends, sales curves, and economic charts along with tables and text. This hardware and software is an asset in a dynamic office where information is the key to success.

Minutes of meetings may be summarized orally, recorded on tape, duplicated, and made immediately available to attendees, who can then take the results of the meeting back to their offices for further study and action. At a recent medical seminar the most popular exhibit on the floor was the booth at which tapes of the sessions were delivered to the hands of physicians ready and willing to hand over $10 for each tape!

These decision-making tools—from hand-held programmable calculators through interactive on-line searching to multimedia displays of information—must be the responsibility of a centralized information department that can coordinate and consolidate requests, to the maximum benefit of the organization.

REFERENCES

1. R. B. Alexander, "Publisher's Memo," *Business Week*, May 14, 1979, p. 6.
2. "The Ombudsmen," *Newsweek*, July 26, 1971, p. 61. Copyright 1971, by Newsweek, Inc. All Rights Reserved. Reprinted by Permission.
3. Tahoe Information & Business Services, Box 4031, Stateline, Nev., 89449.

4

INFORMATION SOURCES

Perhaps paradoxically, as the end users of information grow more confident of their ability to summon what they require from a terminal, there might also be a reduction in corporate staffs and in the use of consultants. In the heaven imagined by data-base pioneers, managers are transfigured from narrow-minded specialists into generalists, with a universe of information literally at their fingertips.[1]

—Walter Kiechel, III

As a manager you must be aware of information sources and services available to you to help improve your decision making, increase your company's productivity, and expand its operations. Ask yourself, "Who knows what I need to know?" Invariably, the answer is, "My information manager."

You have two major sources of information: internal and external.

Internal information ranges in subject matter from accounting data, through personnel records, to zero base budgeting. And your information may be stored in an in-house information center, a personal library, a co-worker's head, or another branch or division of your corporation. As for the medium, it may be a printed page, microfilm, microfiche, computerized data base, audio cassette, videotape, or face-to-face dialog with a colleague. Regardless of location or medium, the crucial fact is that this information has been generated from within your organization. Too often managers seek facts from far afield, forgetting that the information they want may be available in their own "backyard." The alert information manager will install a locator system for pinpointing the person or place most likely to contain the internal information needed. As the information manager, you will set up your own file of important contacts for different types of information. But remember: people and places change. Keep the file current.

Your need for external information opens up an unlimited number of sources that may or may not be physically available to you. The information may be in a textbook, handbook, periodical, or report. Vendor catalogs, government regulations, subcontractor analyses, and outside consultants may also contain the data. Federal, state, regional, and local governments provide in-depth and wideranging information on demographics, census data, economic statistics, environmental information, and data about other companies. Friendly competitors and clients also may prove helpful in providing the information. Trade associations are good sources of information on which you can draw. And there are commercial online information services with instant "fingertip" access to more than 100 data bases containing more than 40,000,000 records. Many of these on-line data bases are abstracting and indexing services that supply bibliographic information about the area of inquiry. Some data bases offer the additional service of document delivery. You simply order the articles you want by commanding your terminal, the data are delivered to you, and you are billed for the items requested. Other data bases identify sources, and you must locate and obtain the documents yourself. There are also factual data bases that give you quantitative answers on the spot. In addition, there are another 400 data bases worldwide that are not generally available to the public, but may be tapped through universities, private organizations, and government agencies.

There are several directories of data bases and information services available. *Computer-Readable Data Bases,* compiled by Martha E. Williams of the University of Illinois, is published by the American Society for Information Science. This directory and data source book describes in detail 528 data bases in 1,400 pages. Cuadra Associates, Inc., in Santa Monica, California, publishes a *Directory of Non-Bibliographic Database Services.* Capital Systems Groups, Inc., in Rockville, Maryland, produces a *Directory of On-Line Information Resources* with a subscription service for updates. *Infor-*

mation Industry Market Place 1981 is published by R. R. Bowker Company and covers machine-readable data bases, information brokers, and information collection and analysis centers, and provides a list of support services and suppliers. *The Directory of Fee-Based Information Services, 1980-1981,* edited by Kelly Warnken, lists information brokers and freelance librarians alphabetically by state and includes subject specializations.

MAKE-OR-BUY DECISIONS

An issue that all managers must consider and that you as an information manager must resolve is whether or not to develop your own computer-based information system. Should you subscribe to one or more of the commercial systems now available? Should you contract with an information broker who will search the various data bases and other sources of information for you? Only one answer is possible: all of the above.

As a manager you have access to internal information that is of a proprietary nature or is competition-sensitive. You want no unauthorized access to that information. And you do not want competitors or developers of potential competitive markets to know you are interested in a particular subject if you are hoping to obtain a patent or develop a new product. Some of this information need not be computerized, but if there are sufficient quantities of such information it may be feasible to transfer it onto magnetic tape, floppy disks, or some other form of machine-readable medium for quick retrieval.

The fact that your organization has a computer should not be the sole criterion for deciding to develop an in-house computerized system. Such a set-up is of little use if you are allowed access infrequently, if your scheduled job gets bumped by higher priorities (such as a payroll run), or if the computer center programmer writes the software packages to suit his convenience rather than meet your needs. That's a shortcut to frustration, anger, and indigestion when you need facts, analyses, and information. Access time, response time, cost, and qualified programmers are important considerations in determining how much of your computerized systems you want in-house.

On-line services and the various masses of information they offer in a multitude of data bases have become a necessary adjunct to today's business person. Data bases are simplistically referred to as either bibliographic or nonbibliographic. Basically, the former are the traditional abstracting and indexing services put into machine-readable form. Nonbibliographic data bases are sometimes referred to as numeric data bases. (This is a slight misnomer because many nonbibliographic data bases offer textual facts as well as numeric statistics.)

Cuadra Associates, in its seminar on nonbibliographic data bases, divides them into two types: reference and source.

Reference data bases comprise bibliographic and referral types of information. Bibliographic data bases contain citations and abstracts to articles, books, reports, and so on. Referral data bases contain leads to individuals, organizations, and technology. Source data bases, on the other hand, provide the actual information being sought.

Source data bases are classified into four types: numeric and statistical; a combination of text and numeric; chemical or physical properties of substances; and full text.

Most data bases available through commercial distributors are primarily bibliographic. But nonbibliographic data bases are becoming increasingly commonplace as contemporary managers see the need for more and varied information to help them make their day-to-day decisions.

In the electronic format, both bibliographic and numeric data bases offer the advantages of speed, lower costs, convenience, and thoroughness. Most importantly, they provide the opportunity for you to interact with the data bases in order to browse, broaden a search, narrow an inquiry, combine concepts, and see the results immediately on a screen and simultaneously printed out at the terminal.

What about the manager who wants access to these data bases but does not have a terminal? For a fee, information brokers will seek out the information manually or electronically in an abstracting and indexing service, locate the document in its repository, obtain a copy or reproduction of the item, and mail or personally deliver the information.

Many companies are too small to install an on-line service in the beginning, and therefore hire information brokers on a contract basis to conduct such services for them. Even companies that have information centers and company libraries may need to hire information brokers at times; for example, when the work load is especially heavy, when the search may require the use of a complex data base, or when the subject is unfamiliar and a specialist from one of the information brokerage houses can search the files more effectively. Many universities have entered the information brokerage business, particularly in the fields of science and technology, as regional dissemination centers for NASA and other government agencies.

Thus the traditional make-or-buy decisions so frequently faced by managers take on different aspects when it comes to that elusive commodity called information. The decision is tripartite: Construct your own in-house information system for internal information or for external information you don't want others to know is of interest to you; purchase access to on-line information data bases through a commercial distributor; or hire the services of an information broker on an as-needed basis or a retainer fee.

COST CONSIDERATIONS

Information is neither free nor cheap. Even so-called "free" information attainable from various government agencies costs you through your ubiquitous taxes. Your taxes pay the salaries of public librarians; your tax money buys the collection of information in various media. Your time and your information manager's time is expensive—even the time you spend seeking out information from so-called "free" sources. The bill mounts when you add long-distance calls (although there are several government agencies and corporations that provide toll-free numbers for your questions).

It is difficult to assign actual dollars and cents to in-house systems. In most cases the computer center's time is considered an overhead cost and you pay the going rate for your company. For all practical purposes, you are dealing in funny money, because you are paying with your department overhead dollars for the services of another overhead function, the computer center. The bottom line shows that the company still foots the bill. There have been cases in which in-house computer costs were so high that the information center, prohibited by charter from owning its own computer, purchased computer services from an outside organization to spin its tapes. This provided the information manager with more overhead dollars to allocate for other information resources.

Several factors determine the costs of the data bases available through information distributors. Two major vendors, Lockheed Information Systems' DIALOG and System Development Corporation's ORBIT, charge by actual usage as measured by (1) how long your terminal is connected with their computers (on-line connect time), (2) off-line printing of the citations and abstracts that the search produces, and (3) communications costs for using Tymnet or Telenet telephone networks. The data bases you search will determine the on-line connect time. Charges for various data bases range from $25 to $125 for each hour of use. Off-line printing rates vary among data bases ranging from 10¢ to $3 for each full record. The cost of communication between your terminal and the distributor's computer is also a variable: Lockheed charges $5 an hour for Telenet, $8 for Tymnet; System Development Corporation charges $8 for either. Both Lockheed and System Development Corporation offer user discounts based on guaranteed minimums, group discounts, and standard contracts for heavy usage.

Bibliographic Retrieval Service (BRS) offers reduced rates for increased usage. Regardless of the data base you select on BRS, the cost may go from $25 per hour (using the system only five hours a month) to $13 per hour (using your terminal 40 or more hours a month). MEDLARS, a medical literature data base produced by the National Library of Medicine, costs a flat rate of $10 per hour no matter how many hours are used.

BRS offers a subscription service costing from $750 annually for up to 25 connect hours to $6,000 per year for up to 480 connect hours. This subscription does not include Telenet communication charges, royalty fees on a half dozen data bases, or off-line print charges, which are fixed at 15¢ a page for all data bases except MEDLARS, which is 12¢ a page.

If all of these various vendors and costs seem complicated, you can use the following formula to evaluate fees: The typical search costs about $1 per minute and it takes 15 to 20 minutes to complete. You will have to figure in additional costs such as your in-house information researcher's time, the time involved in locating the actual document, and the money to reproduce or obtain the information, if you don't already have it in-house.

But consider what it would cost you to hire an information broker. Rates vary and contracts range from a one-shot market survey to a retainer fee for information services. One West Coast information broker charges $25 per hour plus costs, with a two-hour minimum charge for computer and manual searches. If the article or document is in their own files, the basic fee is $4.50 per item plus 15¢ per page; purchases and photocopies from other sources are $7.50 per item plus costs. Current awareness services—where users are automatically notified weekly or monthly about new articles or publications in their fields of interest—may cost $25 to $35 monthly per subject. Preparation of data summaries run $35 per hour. Indexing services may go from $1.25 per entry to $30 per hour.

One information brokerage house on the East Coast operates on a monthly retainer fee. Initially, the retainer is determined in advance based on the types and frequency of questions to be asked. Usually the fee is from $150 to $200 a month. Information requests are monitored to verify that the retainer fee is in line with the amount of time needed to answer your questions. The hourly rate is between $20 and $50, depending on subject matter and complexity. If the total value of the questions is less or more than the retainer fee, the monthly fee is adjusted accordingly for future information services.

SUBJECT COVERAGE

Many managers avoid using computerized data bases because they associate their subject coverage with the fields of science and technology. According to a *Harvard Business Review* article[2] on computerized data bases, authors Darrow and Belilove classify data base content into ten subject areas grouped under three general headings. Under marketing they list *consumer credit; business credit; marketing and demographic statistics.* Under business and finance appear *econometric statistics and modeling; stock, bond, and commodity prices; trading information; corporation statistics;* and *news.* The third heading, bibliographic, comprises *general news abstracts, scientific and technical abstracts, and legal;* and *library.*

ORBIT breaks down its 50-plus data bases into three categories: *science and technology, social science,* and *business.* DIALOG classifies its more than 100 data bases into *science; applied science and technology; social science and humanities;* and *business/economics.*

The problem with classifying data bases by subject matter is that the subject may serve as a blinder to you when you are seeking out information you need, as the following case studies illustrate.

○ Management of a company planning to relocate needs information on various proposed sites. Demographic and census data will give the company this important business information. But the information is not in a business or an economic data base. The information needed is located in a social science and humanities data base, SITE II, a numeric demographic data base.

○ The compensation manager of a major corporation needs information on how to set salaries equitably for employees being sent to Great Britain. This information is found in a numeric data base, Central Statistical Office, produced in England and available as a Chase Econometric data base.

○ Managers of a New England electronics firm want to meet the engineers of a friendly West Coast competitor, but are afraid that they may end up talking with marketing personnel. A scientific and technical data base containing reports published by the company to be visited lists the engineers who wrote the reports. By carefully checking that data base, the New England managers obtain names of the people they really need to speak with.

○ The legal department of a chemical corporation locates the information it needs for litigation support in a medical data base dealing with toxic substances, not in a legal data base.

Thus the sources of information as well as the subject coverage are limited only by the creative imagination of the manager who asks for the information and the information manager who keeps abreast of new sources and subjects.

PRIME USES

Whether you are using manual or computerized sources to obtain information, your information needs can best be described in a temporal way. You want to know what has happened in the past, what is going on now, and what may happen in the future.

Searching past performance is important to finance managers, engineers, marketing directors, production supervisors, personnel departments, and chief executive officers. You want not only to know what you yourself did right in the past, you also want to know what unsuccessful similar projects others undertook so that you do not repeat their errors. Also, analyzing the track records of other companies, products, and people will give you insight as to whether you want to merge with a company, manufacture a new item to replace a product that is losing its share of the market, or evaluate a person you may be considering for your organization. You may conduct a retrospective search, hoping to find nothing (as when an attorney undertakes a patent search to be sure that someone else has not already patented the product or process that a client organization is about to conduct research on and develop).

As a manager you must not only know where you have been, you must know where you are—this helps you know where you're going. Current awareness of internal and external information is necessary for planning, organizing, commanding, coordinating, and controlling. You can keep up to date by reading daily or weekly reports on in-house projects and by consulting computer printouts from external computerized data bases. Managers' fields of interest are profiled, and the subjects searched on the various data bases as they are updated periodically. When a profile interest area and a new entry in the data base match, a printout of the item is made and mailed automatically to the manager. Where the daily business news and current events are vital to a manager's assignments there are data bases that deal primarily with this area, and are updated throughout the day. *Dow Jones News/Retrieval Service* and *The New York Times Information Bank* are examples of systems from which you may get needed information directly, as opposed to using a vendor.

To collect information about the future you don't need to consult your local psychic or blindly "search" your daily horoscope. You do need to access those sources of information that tell what money the government is allocating for research and development, what contracts are being awarded in what areas, and what programs will be phased out. The *Smithsonian Science Information Exchange* data base contains information on current research projects. *Grants Database,* produced by Oryx Press, reports grants offered by government and commercial organizations in 88 subject areas. *PREDICASTS, Inc.,* and other companies report business and economic trends in several forecasting data bases.

Thus managers in the Age of Information can readily locate information that covers past, present, and future activities and put this information to work for profit and progress.

THE INFORMATION INDUSTRY

The following four entities create and handle information as their primary line of business. You must understand these elements if you are to deal effectively with them to fulfill the information needs of your own organization.

Information Producers. These are publishers, data base producers, abstracting and indexing services, compilers of directories, and so on. McGraw-Hill and Doubleday in publishing, Data Courier, Inc., and PREDICASTS, Inc., in data base production, professional societies and their associated abstracting and indexing services, and R. R. Bowker Company and Gale Research in directories are the backbone of information producers. Computer-aided production of directories, newspapers, and abstracting and indexing services makes it possible for print publishers to expand into the areas of data base production. The data base industry is a lucrative field. In 1976 the revenue level was estimated at $740 million. It grew to $1.1 billion by 1980 and predictions are that it will soar to $1.6 billion by 1985.

Information Distributors. These are book and journal wholesalers, on-line services, and libraries with interlibrary loan systems. As mentioned earlier, the three major distributors of on-line services are Lockheed Information Services' DIALOG, System Development Corporation's ORBIT, and Bibliographic Retrieval Service's BRS. But in some cases the distributor of the data base is the publisher itself. For example, *Dow Jones News/Retrieval* is available directly from Dow Jones and Company, publishers of *The Wall Street Journal* and *Barron's*. *The New York Times Information Bank* is also obtained only through its publisher. Data Resources, Incorporated (DRI), is also a major on-line service for nonbibliographic data bases such as those published by The Conference Board and Value Line.

In 1979, Otto Eckstein, chairman of DRI, sold his business to McGraw-Hill, Inc., for $103 million. This seems to herald a movement by giant information corporations to reinforce their positions in the Age of Information.

Information Retailers. These are the so-called information brokers that provide search services and the specialized research companies that conduct market surveys and industry analyses and make economic projections. Also included are those organizations and consultants that will help you determine which equipment is best for your information needs. These information retailers do not supplant your information manager and his organization; rather they support the information resource management operation within your company. Many retailers are listed in the Information Industry Association's annual *Information Sources,* in *The Directory of*

Fee-Based Information Services by Kelly Warnken, and in R. R. Bowker's *Information Industry Market Place.*

Information Systems, Technologies, and Equipment. IBM, Control Data Corporation, Xerox, and AT&T are the types of companies that dominate this element. They provide you with the hardware to control the spate of information that affects every organization in the private and public sector. Computers, micrographic equipment, text processing, communications systems, and computer-aided graphic arts are the tools that symbolize the Age of Information. The $11 billion market for microelectronics alone is expected to increase 20 percent annually over the next five years.

Managers of successful companies here and abroad are fast realizing that someone must take over the responsibilities of coordinating and directing the information needs of their organizations. The person assigned this task is called the information manager and his is a complex and demanding responsibility. Eighty percent of the total information resources of a company are produced in-house; 20 percent are acquired from other sources. Your information manager must establish policies and procedures to maximize your company's utilization of an important economic resource: information.

REFERENCES

1. Walter Kiechel, III, "Everything You Always Wanted to Know May Soon Be On-Line," *Fortune,* May 5, 1980, p. 240. © 1980 Time Inc. All rights reserved.
2. Joel W. Darrow and James R. Belilove, "The Growth of Databank Sharing," *Harvard Business Review,* November–December 1978, pp. 180–194.

Part II:
Manageable Information

5

INFORMATION AS A RESOURCE

We are at the dawn of the era of the smart machine—an "information" age that will change forever the way an entire nation works, plays, travels and even thinks. Just as the industrial revolution dramatically expanded the strength of man's muscles and the reach of his hand, so the smart-machine revolution will magnify the power of his brain. But unlike the industrial revolution, which depended on finite resources such as iron and oil, the new information age will be fired by a seemingly limitless resource— the inexhaustible supply of the knowledge itself.[1]

—Newsweek, *June 30, 1980*

Individuals, organizations, and nations must consider information as a basic resource, a resource having the same degree of importance as other forms of matter and energy. Information is not free. But, in a positive sense, information has inestimable value.

INFORMATION—AN ECONOMIC RESOURCE

Information is like oil. Prospecting and exploration of oil can be compared to determining the best source of information. Drilling and completing wells is analogous to developing search strategies. Recovery of oil is similar to retrieving the raw data. The crude oil must be refined and processed; data must be analyzed and synthesized (into information). Oil storage and the problem of transporting it are not too different from the problems of maintaining and disseminating information to the ultimate user. The oil–information analogy may be carried even further when we consider that there are various grades of oil just as there are various grades of information. And just as the cost of oil has soared in the past few years, so too has the price of information increased.

However, there are some basic differences between information and other resources. Information is not depleted when it is retrieved. It loses nothing in quantity, content, power, or value. As a matter of fact, value is added as information is used. Also, information is not consumed or destroyed when it is put to use. One item of information may be used indefinitely. Information is indeed the ideal asset. But a note of caution: Although information may not be depleted or destroyed by usage, it may become obsolete.

Harvard University's Program on Information Resources Policy succinctly describes information as a resource that is critical for managing other basic resources.

> "Information Resources" is a concept like energy resources. Both of these resources are fundamental to the well-being of individuals and organizations in today's world.
>
> As with energy, politics and technology are changing the ways in which information is produced, stored, communicated, processed, and used. No crisis like the Arab oil embargo has dramatized the implications of these changes. Yet, they are real and at hand.
>
> Indeed most organizations are sensitive, even vulnerable to change, for they—in some cases without as yet realizing it—are spending a substantial portion of their operating budgets on "information resources" to effectively and efficiently conduct their operations.[2]

Walter M. Carlson, corporate marketing consultant for IBM Corporation, spotlighted information as an economic resource in his keynote address at the Annual Meeting of the American Society for Information Science in 1977. He stated, "The one central fact which will control the management of information in the 1980s is that information conserves other resources through better decisions."[3]

He went on to summarize where the payoff areas lie.

> At the national level, we need new stimuli to improve productivity. We need it to maintain growth and a competitive trade position in the world's economy. Our nation also needs to remain competitive in such

vital areas as national security. In the 1980s our ability to manage the flow of information to this country's leaders will be a critical determinant in the position the U.S. holds in the world order.

Our organizations in both the public and private sectors are constantly in search for better ways to reduce costs and to meet the demands of a growing economy without too large an expenditure of resources. They are also committed to improving their products or services to remain competitive and grow. The management of the flow of information to an organization's decision-makers and from them to the implementers of their decisions is still an art form. We have just begun to understand the underlying structure of this information flow. At the personal level, we seek information to help do our job better, to improve our own or our group's productivity, and to make better decisions.[4]

In the public sector the federal government has also recognized that information is an economic resource. The 96th Congress' Bill H.R. 4572 is a proposed revision of Title 44 of the U.S. Code that regulates printing, publishing, and disseminating government documents through the Government Printing Office. Its Section 1101 reads as follows:

Information resource managers. (a) The head of each department, agency and entity of the government shall designate from among the officers and employees of such an entity an information resources manager. . . . (b) Each information resources manager appointed under subsection (a) of this section shall report directly to, and be under the direction of the head of, the department, agency, or entity involved, and shall not be under the control of, or subject to supervision by, any other person.

Another indication of information as an indispensable economic resource with great value to our society is seen by the increase in the number of information-related crimes. Frauds, embezzlements, kickbacks, and questionable accounting practices in business, industry, and government are making headlines every day. The computer and calculator have been added to the gun and knife as weapons in the criminal's arsenal.

As Marvin E. Wolfgang, director of the Center for Studies in Criminality and Criminal Law, University of Pennsylvania, reports:

> Part of this change is already being reflected in a new form of information or knowledge theft that is becoming a major type of criminality. Computer tape theft, computer program theft, and corporate information burglary are styles of crime that are already prominent. The theft of information in order to obtain positions of power will increase. The Pentagon Papers, the attempt to steal information from Daniel Ellsberg's psychiatrist, the entire Watergate scandal are among the more dramatic illustrations of this kind of theft.[5]

Possibly the ultimate acknowledgment of information as an economic resource occurred in 1978 when The Royal Swedish Academy of Sciences awarded Herbert A. Simon the Nobel Prize for economics. In *Administrative Behavior,* Simon challenged the prevalent theories of decision making, which held that managers made their decisions to maximize profits based on complete information acquired at no cost. Simon contended,

> While economic man maximizes—selects the best alternative from among all those available to him; his cousin, whom we shall call administrative man, satisfices [sic]—looks for a course of action that is satisfactory or 'good enough.' Examples of satisficing criteria that are familiar enough to businessmen, if unfamiliar to most economists, are "share of market," "adequate profit," "fair price."[6]

He explained the reasons for satisficing as follows:

> It is impossible for the behavior of a single, isolated individual to reach any high degree of rationality. The number of alternatives he must explore is so great, the information he would need to evaluate them so vast that even an approximation to objective rationality is hard to conceive. Individual choice takes place in an environment of "givens"— premises that are accepted by the subject as bases for his choice; and behavior is adaptive only within the limits set by these "givens."[7]

Simon summed up his economic achievements when the award was announced. "The work that I did tried to take into account limits on people's ability to compute and deal with incomplete information and sometimes overwhelming information."

The Business of Information

In addition to information brokerage businesses that gather information for individuals and organizations, there are many groups whose primary economic structure is based on information. Examples are the international news-gathering services such as the Associated Press and United Press International and the daily newspapers that deal in only one commodity: information. Specialized information services such as the Dow Jones News Wire and business periodicals like *The Wall Street Journal* and *Business Week* offer the same product to the business world. The publishing houses, particularly those printing textbooks and nonfiction material, are all businesses based on information. The polling organizations such as The Roper Organization, Inc., Louis Harris and Associates, Inc., and the Gallup Organization, Inc., are names familiar to most Americans. They, too, produce, package, and sell one product: information.

There are also think tanks. Webster's New Collegiate Dictionary (1980) defines a think tank as "an institute, corporation, or group organized for interdisciplinary research (as in technological and social problems)—called also *think factory.*" But this definition is limited in scope. According to a Library of Congress report, "In its narrowest definition, think tanks are engaged in the study of policy alternatives and recommendations—'policy research.' The term, though, can be applied broadly to those think tanks which engage in advanced technology development and systems engineering."[8] These think tanks can be classified into three types: nonprofit (which constitutes the majority), for-profit, and government-sponsored.

Two major think tanks are the Brookings Institution and the American Enterprise Institute for Public Policy Research (AEI). Both are nonprofit, nonpartisan private organizations that act as disinterested third parties. Brookings is considered liberal-oriented and calls upon the counsel of many Democrats who formerly held important government jobs. AEI tends to be conservative and uses the services of former Republican officials. Among the people who act as consultants for these think tanks are men and women who made headlines because of policy decisions they made while in office. Former Federal Reserve Board chairman Arthur Burns, director of the Council on Wage and Price Stability Barry P. Bosworth, and former Treasury Secretary William E. Simon are among some of these luminaries. They are the "in-and-outers" of government, for the party in power determines whose proposition holds sway.

No matter which party is in office, many of the recommendations in the studies and reports published by these two think tanks find their way into official government policies that affect you as managers. According to a *U.S. News & World Report* article, "Policymakers often turn directly to Brookings or AEI for counsel. Phone calls are made daily from administration officials and congressional staffs to the eight-story Brookings headquarters on Washington's Embassy Row and to AEI's two rented floors in a downtown office building."[9]

Some 35,000 management consulting firms sell information for a profit. They do not limit their services to the private sector. For example, Arthur D. Little, the biggest in the business, is listed as a think tank by the Congressional Research Service of the Library of Congress.

The trend in management consulting is toward specialization. As Joseph J. Brady, executive vice president of the Association of Consulting Management Engineers, is quoted as stating, "Consulting is booming because the world is getting more complex. Things are changing so rapidly that companies want specialists to come in and help."[10] Many CPA firms such as Peat, Marwick, Mitchell; Ernst & Whinney; and Price Waterhouse are the leaders in management consulting. They have had many years of experience in dealing with information and information systems in business operations. The management advisory services they offer are now an extension of their expertise into the fields of market research and strategic planning.

As demands for information are increasing, many organizations have become specialists in selling information on how to process it. The $200 million market for information on information processing, for example, is growing by about 20 percent annually. And management consulting firms like Arthur D. Little and Booz

Allen and Hamilton have taken the lead in producing research and consulting on information processing.

The business world generally, and managers specifically, are beginning to realize that information is an economic resource they can tap, produce, package, and sell. Corporations need information to compete, grow, and profit, and companies are being formed to fill that need for information. The manager who fails to focus on the information needs of his company will soon be bypassed by a new breed of managers who realize that information is the lifeblood of the corporate body.

INFORMATION—A PERSONAL RESOURCE

The concept of information as a personal resource with great value to the individual is recognized in Article 1, Section 8, of The Constitution of the United States. "The Congress shall have power to promote the progress of science and useful arts, by securing for limited times to authors and inventors the exclusive right to their respective writings and discoveries." The Founding Fathers, in the framework of an agricultural milieu, had the vision and foresight to realize the paramount importance of an individual's information and its economic value then and now.

The information you possess, your know-how, your expertise, and your ability to put that information to use in business determine your economic worth and status within a company. You have made a major investment in time pursuing the acquisition of information: twelve years of public school, probably four years of college, and perhaps an additional two or more years of graduate work. You and your parents have invested tens of thousands of dollars to prepare you with the information you need to enter, compete in, and grow in the business world. Information gathering must continue for you to maintain your position and to advance.

You must know who you are and what you have to sell before you can market your abilities and potentialities to a prospective employer. Very often it is not what you know but whom you know. Contacts and information sources have value in the information marketplace. To better know yourself, you must take stock of what you have to offer. Construct a personal inventory of the information that you have that is needed in today's business world. List these information assets in a descending order of worth. Don't stop there. Analyze the list, noting carefully what essential information is missing. Then take the necessary steps to bring your information inventory up to full capacity. Some of your information shortages can be filled quickly; in other areas you will need more time.

In preparing your personal information inventory, consider shrinkage. How applicable is some of the information you now possess in today's information-based business world? How much of what you once learned do you now remember? Times have changed. Where colleges once required competency in a foreign language before a degree was granted, competency in computer language is now a requirement in many undergraduate schools.

Business and industry spend about $2 billion annually on education to keep their employees current with the latest information. Eighty percent of that $2 billion is expended on in-house company education and training services, according to a study conducted by The Conference Board.[11] Continuing education, either through in-house programs, on-campus schooling, or attendance at professional meetings and seminars, add to your personal information worth—to yourself and to your organization. Not only must you keep aware of changing knowledge and technology, you must continually add to your information inventory. This is the only way you can be prepared to assume new responsibilities and improve performance in your present assignment.

Another kind of information to consider is experience-derived information. There is on-the-job training that bolsters your information inventory totals, and there are social, political, and personal activities from which you have developed information resources that may be used in your business undertakings. When writing your resume, take note that personnel administrators prefer to see your work experience listed before your education—they consider the years of work more meaningful to an evaluation of your worth to their company.

Add to your personal information inventory the number of articles you have published, books you have written, patents you have been awarded, and speeches you have delivered. These accomplishments display you as an information-oriented individual who has ideas to sell, concepts to develop, and talents to market.

How valuable are you as an information resource to a firm? A dollars-and-cents value has to be based on the going rate for different career categories. When you add up your information worth you must consider the supply-and-demand factors that determine what the market will pay for that kind of information. But don't sell yourself short. A bonus has to be added to cover your potential for information enrichment. This must be factored into the formula that prices the information in your head. Information is indeed a valuable resource for yourself and your employer. It is the one thing you have to sell in the information-oriented world of business that dominates today's economy.

INFORMATION—AN ORGANIZATIONAL RESOURCE

In the Industrial Age the resources of a company or corporation could be reduced to two basic elements: labor and capital. Today, economists, corporate executives, and managers are realizing that there is a third essential resource an organization must have: information.

You as a manager must use your organization's information resources for problem solving and decision making. Information is at the core of creative thinking, which leads to new ways of improving products, processes, and services, to the invention of new devices, and to the discovery of new, marketable concepts. Thus the information resources of your organization have a dual application: for internal operations and external marketing potential.

Management literature amply describes the techniques of using information internally to integrate and coordinate the various elements that make up an organization. The information that is used to achieve corporate goals may be based on past performance, derived by deductive or inductive analysis of existing data, or gathered from customers, competitors, and government regulations and through scientific and technical breakthroughs. Forecasting techniques provide you with information as to the possibility/probability of future environments that may cause significant shifts in consumer demand, the economy, social and cultural change, and potential competition. You need information to determine profitable and socially conscious objectives and to meet these goals.

The information resource that makes your business a success can also be marketed for a profit by other companies, government bodies, and foreign outlets. The ingenuity, know-how, and proven capabilities that you have spent years perfecting are salable commodities in the world marketplace, as are the products and services that your business sells. Rather than investing huge capital expenditures in building overseas plants that may some day be nationalized, many corporations now adopt a less risky and more profitable method: technology transfer. They sell the plans and know-how to overseas and domestic businesses. A growing number of companies are preparing information packages and assembling a coterie of experts: They sell know-how and the consultants' management abilities at a high return on investment with a low expenditure of funds.

The current trend is to sell proprietary information, not products. In the past, American enterprises marketed fully developed technologies to foreign buyers. This method required a heavy investment in capital and labor, and required the continuing presence of American technicians and managers to operate and direct the plants. Such an arrangement fostered the resentment of less-developed countries. Today, foreign governments and companies are willing and eager to acquire technology through licensing. You as a manager can profit from investments in research and development and the resulting products and services, and then make a secondary return on that same investment through licensing the information. Your management skills are now shifting from a capital- and labor-intensive operation to an information-intensive one.

How do you find out who is willing to buy your know-how? Who wants to purchase your information at home and overseas? Technotec, a technology exchange service of Control Data Corporation, maintains a data base containing information supplied by customers from all over the world, listing the technology that is needed, the technology that is available, and the experts who can help transfer the technology. In essence, it is a computerized matching of buyer and seller in the information marketplace. Licensable Technology, a data base compiled by Dr. Dvorkovitz and Associates, lists more than 20,000 items available for licensing. Trade Opportunities is an international marketing data base that provides leads to export opportunities for U.S. business. This data base contains more than 70,000 records on direct sales leads in more than 120 countries. It is updated weekly with about 500 entries per week. The U.S. Foreign Service collects the information from around the world and supplies it to the U.S. Department of Commerce, which prepares the data base.

Your information manager can access these data bases and suggest additional sources of information so that you can profit from your most valuable organization resource—information.

Information Indicators

Taking a cue from the 12 leading economic indicators that show trends in the overall business cycle of the economy, alert managers and business executives should establish "personalized" information indicators for their own company to determine how well the organization is performing in an information-competitive economy.

Naturally, each industry will have its own unique information indicators, and each business will have certain information elements that are peculiar to its particular endeavors. However, some general indicators will give you an insight into how "healthy" (with respect to information) your organization is. By acting promptly and positively in response to these signals, you will soon see results: increased productivity, expansion of the market share of your organization, and stimulated efficiency through innovation, diversification, and growth.

The number of patents pending or issued to employees of your company is substantive evidence of how well your organization is putting information to work. The patented product opens up opportunities for increased sales, new jobs, and potential profits. Industry leaders encourage their engineers and scientists to come up with inventions and obtain patents. These patents can be used initially by the company, then licensed for further return on investments.

The number of copyrighted reports, books, technical articles, and other written or recorded material in an organization's technical information center indicates how information-oriented a corporation is. The author-employees publish innovative concepts that translate into profits for the company.

Oral presentations and public addresses made by informed, authoritative employees are also indicators of an organization that takes a positive approach toward information. The speeches may be sales presentations that result in new customers, more orders, and expanded services—with a bottom line that adds up to better community relations, increased recognition of the company as a leader in the industry, and a greater awareness by the public that profit is a five-letter word that benefits all.

The number of employees who belong to professional societies is yet another quantitative measure of information trends in your organization. It indicates to you how well your professional staff is keeping current by reading the journals, technical papers, and other publications produced and distributed by these societies.

The professional seminars, meetings, and trade shows that your employees attend indicate the extent to which they are exposed to the latest technology and thinking that is so vital to your company's well-being. Attendance at meetings is important from the aspect of learning from formal presentations given, but the personal contacts your employees establish with professional peers is also valuable, as they may result in scientific, technical, and managerial enrichment.

A count of new products and services offered by your organization is still another indicator of how well informed your company is. These products and services, the results of information gathering, analyzing, synthesizing, and shaping into ideas, culminate into tangible, salable items.

An effective and efficient in-house information system will provide your employees with technical and management information that can help them improve their job performance. The current status and the availability of your collection of internal and external reports and the number of data bases your information center can tap and how frequently they are used are information indicators that the alert manager will watch.

These quantitative information indicators are merely suggestions. You will want to expand this list and modify it to your company's specific functions. However, information indicators will help you to better assess your current information status and evaluate the future of your company. After-the-fact statistics tell you only where you have been—something you can do nothing about.

Protecting Information

Information is an organizational resource that must be protected. Managers are fast realizing that information is one of the most sought-after and expensive commodities in the business world. In an information-sensitive marketplace, the security of your information is of major concern.

There are three legal ways to protect your intellectual property: copyright, patent, and trade secret. Under the Copyright Law of 1978, the author or copyright holder can legally monopolize the market for his original work from the date of creation of the work to 50 years after his death. Corporate authorship permits a copyright duration of 75 years from date of publication or 100 years from date of creation, whichever is shorter. But the copyright protects only the author's expression, not the information or facts themselves. With the proliferation of copying machines in our business society, a main concern of the new law is to determine if a copy may be made by "fair use" or if it infringes rights. Four points decide the question of "fair use":

1. Whether or not the copy is made for commercial gain or non-profit use.
2. What the nature of the work being copied is.
3. What percentage of work is being copied.
4. What results copying will have on the commercial market.

Patents give inventors the same thing that copyrights grant authors: a monopoly over the manufacture and sale of their products for a specific period of time. In the case of patents the period is 17 years. To file for and prosecute a patent costs about $4,000 and the patent may take up to four years to acquire. If you file patent applications in foreign countries, you must pay the same fee to each country in which you file.

Trade secrets, which include information not generally known in the industry that gives one business an advantage over another, have no statutory laws governing them, but are protected by common law. Trade secrets can be lost in two ways: they may be stolen or a company may hire a key person from another organization who brings the secret with him. One way to prevent a brain drain from revealing your trade secrets is to have all new employees sign an employment agreement specifying certain types of information that cannot be disclosed, under penalty of law. Companies that are involved in joint ventures must sometimes divulge secret information to each other. In these areas, it is essential to identify the proprietary data and clearly stipulate the conditions of divulgence.

How long can a company really keep a secret? The recipe for Coca-Cola has been guarded by the company for more than 75 years beyond the date that a patent would have expired.

Electronic safeguards for information need also be considered. With so much information being computerized today, you as a manager must ensure that computer security procedures are established to prevent disclosure of the contents of the computer files. The computer's vulnerability is well documented and computer crimes have become so common they no longer receive front-page position in the newspapers. Obviously, physical protection of computer hardware can be assured through locks and guards. But it is building security into the various programs that is essential to secure your information. One way is to identify the user. Passwords or secret numbers are frequently used for this. After identification, be sure that the person is authorized access to that particular file. A precaution that must definitely be built into the system is protection of the integrity of a file. Some system must be established to verify that a person making changes has authorization to alter the contents of a file, and also a record must be made of what changes have been made.

Each company must assess its information holdings and exercise protective measures to safeguard that asset. The information manager must work in concert with the security department, data processing organization, and legal division to come up with a viable system to protect the company's "knowledge bank."

INFORMATION—A NATIONAL RESOURCE

Just as information is a personal and organizational resource, it is also a national resource. President Carter stated in 1979,

Information, like the air we breathe, is a national resource. Accurate and useful information is as necessary as oxygen to our health and happiness as individuals and as a nation. More than half of our gross national product now comes from activity related to information. Information is rapidly replacing manufactured goods as a major commodity in our economy.

It often supplies the vital spark for innovation in our Nation's business, science, law, medicine, government and technology. It lights fires of creative genius and invention and thus helps solve the problems of an increasingly complex world.[12]

In spite of presidential recognition of the importance of information to the American economy, no national information policy exists. Unless such a policy is forthcoming, Americans and American businesses may find themselves in a precarious position in the world economy.

As rich in information as the United States seems, it is not self-sufficient. For example, American research libraries now receive 60 percent of their new material from foreign sources. According to a December 1978 government report on information policy, two-thirds of all research and development is now conducted in foreign laboratories. Information is a critical resource in conducting foreign policy and is a vital element of American business operations at home and abroad.

American enterprise can prosper in this new economic world if it is responsive to the demands and needs for various kinds of information. Today we talk of petrodollars; the concept of "infodollars" will very soon become a reality.

As the comptroller general of the United States reported to Congress in 1979, "The federal government needs to recognize the value of scientific, technical, and other specialized information it produces and take steps to manage it as carefully as it does other valuable resources."[13]

China offers an excellent example of how crucial information is as a national resource. When I visited China in 1978, the country had just embarked on its program to move from an agricultural society into an industrial economy; China plans to enter the Age of Information by the year 2000. Deng Xiaoping (Teng Hsiaoping), China's vice premier, has called upon the one billion Chinese people to participate in "the four modernizations"—improvements in agriculture, industry, science and technology, and defense. The infrastructure of this four-point program is information.

There is developing in China today a new middle class based on education and access to information. When U.S. Commerce Secretary Juanita Kreps visited China in May 1979, she presented China's foreign trade minister Li Qiang with an information system (produced by Information Handling Services) capable of providing data on 10 million products of 15,000 U.S. manufacturers and distributors. This microfiche system is updated every two months and sells for $22,000. China has also acquired access to *Chemical Abstracts'* computerized data base and *Engineering Index's* computer-readable files, and in August 1980 China established its own school of business administration, with the help of the U.S. Department of Commerce. Among its embryo faculty, all from the United States, are academicians from such disciplines as information systems, economics, accounting, and management. Mr. Deng's mandate for speeding economic development, improving productivity, and increasing profitability is an information-driven program that is well under way in post-Mao China.

The American manager must realize that international information transfer is a multilateral phenomenon of which he is a part. The successful manager views information as a personal, organizational, and national resource. This attitude will be profitable to him, his organization, and the nation if he properly plans, budgets, and audits this renewable resource.

REFERENCES

1. "Machines That Think," *Newsweek,* June 30, 1980, p. 50. Copyright 1980, by Newsweek, Inc. All Rights Reserved. Reprinted by Permission.

2. *Information Resources: Performance, Profits and Policy,* Program on Information Resources Policy (Cambridge, Mass.: Harvard University, n.d.), p. 5.

3. Walter M. Carlson, "Where Is the Payoff?" *Bulletin of the American Society for Information Science,* Vol. 4, No. 1 (October 1977), p. 14.

4. *Ibid.,* pp. 14–15.

5. Marvin E. Wolfgang, "Rethinking Crime and Punishment," *Across the Board,* September 1978, p. 59. Reprinted by permission of Daedalius, *Journal of the American Academy of Arts and Sciences,* Winter 1978, Boston, Mass.

6. Herbert A. Simon, *Administrative Behavior,* 2nd ed. (New York: The Free Press, 1957), p. *xxv.*

7. *Ibid.,* p. 79.

8. Elizabeth J. Guarisco, *Think Tanks—What Are They and What Do They Do?*" Report 76-1835P, Congressional Research Service, Library of Congress, Washington, D.C., October 4, 1976, p. 4.

9. "Two 'Think Tanks' with Growing Impact," *U.S. News & World Report,* September 25, 1978, p. 47. © 1978.

10. "The New Shape of Management Consulting," *Business Week,* May 21, 1979, p. 99.

11. Seymour Lusterman, *Education in Industry,* The Conference Board Report No. 719, 1977, p. 12.

12. "Message from the President," *The White House Conference on Library and Information Services,* November 15–19, 1979, Program Book, n.d., n.p.

13. *Better Information Management Policies Needed: A Study of Scientific and Technical Bibliographic Services,* Comptroller General's Report to Congress, Report PSAD-79-62, U.S. General Accounting Office, Washington, D.C., August 6, 1979, p. *i.*

6

PLANNING, BUDGETING, AND AUDITING INFORMATION RESOURCES

By budgeting for information, the cost of information be-
comes visible. *Being visible, it is a subject of scrutiny and
the efforts of the planner are more closely and carefully
directed to collect only that information absolutely necessary. As the concept of Information Resources Management becomes more established in planning and budgeting
processes, much "just in case" data should be eliminated.*[1]
—*Forest Woody Horton, Jr.*

Business, industry, and government need to plan, budget, and audit
information needs just as they audit the needs of any other resource
within their organizations.

PLANNING

A major objective in resource planning is to identify resource
needs early enough so that they will be available when needed. Although information is invisible, elusive, and changeable, you can
and must undertake long-range plans for it.

As new businesses emerge and government agencies are formed
in our post-industrial society, information planning must be a fore-
thought, not an afterthought. The creation of the Department of
Energy exemplifies this new line of management thinking very well.
When Dr. James R. Schlesinger organized the twelfth cabinet
agency in 1977, one of the 14 executive levels reporting directly to
him was the Energy Information Administration. A specific person
and a definite organization were assigned responsibility for admin-
istering a central, comprehensive, and unified information program.

According to the Department of Energy Organization Act (Public Law 95-91) the four major functions of the Energy Information Administration are (1) data collection and processing, (2) data validation, (3) applied analysis, and (4) information management and dissemination. This long-range planning for information needs for and at the highest level of government is indicative of management's recognition of information's importance.

Systematic management of information is vital to your firm's operation. The information may be externally generated or internally developed—the areas of information may deal with products, production, consumers, marketing, and so on, depending on the nature of the business or industry. This information, in turn, is the basis for your corporation's strategic planning, as well as its operations planning and research and development planning. Thus the successful corporation plans for information, and uses that information in its planning.

Embedded in the need for information planning is the fact that organizational policies, goals, and objectives must be met. These policies may vary among companies, but there are universal policies that can be related directly to the various stakeholders your organization will be dealing with:

○ Customers expect high-quality products and services, products that are reliable and fairly priced. (In the case of government organizations or not-for-profit institutions the constituents are the customers.)

○ Employees expect decent salaries and benefits, the opportunity for advancement, and a good physical and psychological working environment.

○ Shareholders expect a satisfactory return on their investment.

○ The community expects you to operate as a responsible corporate citizen, maintaining an attractive facility, supporting deserving projects, and hiring employees who will be an asset to the community.

○ The government (federal, state, regional, and local) expects you to obey laws and regulations.

○ Suppliers expect you to act in a fair and reasonable way in awarding contracts for their goods and services.

○ Dealers expect you to supply them equitably and quickly, and to help them promote and sell your product or service.

○ Competitors expect you to operate fairly and honestly in a free enterprise market.

There are other stakeholders that your particular company may do business with, such as educators, members of the armed forces, and political groups. Of course, you will establish policies, goals, and objectives that deal with these specific publics.

Regardless of which stakeholders are germane to your organization, your company needs information to fulfill their expectations and to gain their support. Without an integrated information network, expectations may sour into frustrations. Information cannot be obtained on an as-needed basis. It must be planned for. Information is not static; it is as changeable as the people who constitute the various stakeholder groups. Information collection, processing, and dissemination is an on-going system in a viable organization.

Every company needs information to exist, grow, and reach its full potential through efficient and effective operations. Your company is no exception. To achieve these critical elements of survival, development, and accomplishment, your company depends on current information to determine where it stands in the competitive marketplace, where management would like it to be in the near and distant future (short- and long-term goals), and what plans and alternatives managers must make to attain these objectives.

Thus the information needs you must plan for fall into two categories: external and internal. Externally, you must keep abreast of what is happening economically, politically, and socially at home and abroad. Your information department can locate, access, and deliver these data for you. But it cannot be done on an "if I wanted it tomorrow I would have asked for it tomorrow" basis. These kinds of data go beyond the information gleaned from reading the current business periodicals and trade journals to get a feel for international and national states of affairs. They call for digging into data bases to reveal demographic trends, tracking competitors' activities, and maintaining constant surveillance of changing customers' needs. Without a firm evaluation of what your company's external information needs are, you will be gathering inconsequential information that hampers corporate decision making—or, worse, formulating policies and plans that have no sound basis in the real world of business.

Information that you require is undoubtedly already being generated within your organization as part of its normal operations. The problems are usually that the information is not being systematically maintained or is not in a format that is useful to you. Or, the information may not be readily available to other managers within the organization and there may be no central organization that can either retrieve portions from the various information locations or refer people to these areas.

In today's information-based business world what is needed is a comprehensive information plan. Such a plan should consist of five steps.

First, scan and monitor the information industry to note trends in data base production, information-related hardware, and pricing. Use your observations to develop long-, medium-, and short-range plans for your information requirements. Trying to predict conditions that will exist 20 years hence seems futile in an industry in which technological breakthroughs occur almost daily. Stay flexible. Remember, your plan is not chiseled in granite; it must be flexible enough to accommodate changes. How will national and international affairs affect your access to information? We are already seeing information barriers being erected to hamper the flow of data among nations. Our government is opening up more of its files on scientific and technical information to promote technology transfer at home. Observing economic and social trends reveals the types of information that may soon be needed to take advantage of opportunities, foil threats, and operate a viable organization.

After you have determined information trends, your second step is to assess the information needs of your company. What are the special needs of the manufacturing department, research and development division, marketing area, and so on? Next list the priorities of the information needs of these various segments. For example, when a new product or service is being developed, greater information support should be extended to the engineering or research and development elements of your organization. As the product or service has been developed, it is probable that greater information needs will be required by the manufacturing and marketing divisions. As the company shifts into a production-oriented mode, the professional and industrial relations division will perhaps need information regarding personnel selection and training programs to fill new jobs.

The third element of effective planning for information is the development of methods to locate and acquire the information for users. This is when the information resources of your organization acquire shape and direction. As mentioned earlier, the information resources will change as the course of your organization shifts—and you must remain alert and responsive to these changes. Also, information that was once inaccessible to you may now be readily available to your organization.

The fourth segment of your information plan requires an evaluation of your information resources and an assessment of how effectively and efficiently you are using these resources to attain corporate goals. What services should be discontinued? What new areas should be added? Are the information resources being integrated into the overall operations of the company? Such questions must be addressed and answered with appropriate corrective actions taken as needed.

The fifth area of information planning requires review and updating of plans. What new opportunities have occurred that demand information support? What competitive threats have emerged that require a reevaluation of information products and services? What shifts in government policies mandate a new approach to your information handling methods? This brings you back to the first element of information planning where the cycle begins once again.

John F. Rockart, at M.I.T.'s Sloan School of Management, has looked at the ways managers plan for their information needs today; he has found them wanting.[2] The current and predominant method is what he calls a "by-product technique." In this approach, top management gets its information as a spin-off from reports and computer runs that are needed for their everyday operation of the business. The result is a deluge of information, much of it irrelevant to the managers' needs. There is the null approach, an informal information system in which executives depend on oral and subjective information to handle situations as they arise. A glamorous method that is fast gaining popularity is the key indicator system. In this system managers determine key indicators, report exceptions to these critical items, and usually display the information graphically. In the total study process, managers examine the information systems that exist in the organization and, through a broad sampling of middle managers, identify the information gaps that need filling. This method is comprehensive but expensive.

Rockart suggests a new systems technique for chief executives to use to determine their own information needs: a "critical success factors" approach. He defines critical success factors as those areas in which good performance is needed to attain the organization's goals. By monitoring and controlling these factors through both quantitative and qualitative information, the probability of meeting the goals increases significantly.

Planning your information needs thus requires creativity and flexibility, for it is through your information assets that you manage all the other assets of your organization.

BUDGETING

There must be a financial commitment for information facilities, equipment, staff, and products if your organization is to function effectively in this new era. You must understand thoroughly your present level of expenditure for information in your own organization, and its rate of growth or decline. Your budget will be based on your plan, and a sound plan will identify the level and timing of your information resources. As with any other resource, actual usage will be matched to the plan and any variance identified. Control of information expenditures dictates that your reporting system will indicate any major changes between actual and planned expenditures, allowing time for corrective action.

Budgets deal with the economic resources of an organization. Information is one of those resources. Thus your budget needs to translate your operating information plan into accounting language.

Since information demands and outputs are so variable, the most effective form of cost control is the flexible budget that allows for changes. However, your organization may mandate the budgetary method for you. This is particularly true in public administration. For example, under President Lyndon B. Johnson, the Planning-Programming-Budgeting System (PPBS) became the administrative device for the entire federal structure. In PPBS the emphasis is on the output of the various programs rather than on the input of expenditures. But as enthusiastic as President Johnson was in implementing the program throughout his administration, he wrote the following:

> It is important to remember one thing: no system, no matter how refined, can make decisions for you. You and I have that responsibility in the executive branch. But our judgment is no better than our information. This system will present us with the alternatives and the information on the basis of which we can, together, make better decisions. The people will be the beneficiary. . . .[3]

Under the Carter Administration, zero base budgeting (ZBB) became the preferred budgeting technique for the federal government, and many business firms are revising their budgeting systems to use the ZBB approach. Under ZBB you must justify each item annually before it can be included in the budget.

Many businesses and government agencies would prefer to plan and budget their information needs incrementally—taking last year's spending levels and adding to or subtracting from them. However, you can apply ZBB techniques successfully to handle your information needs.

The main element of a zero base budget is the decision package. This is a brief description of a discrete function that is carried out in support of a major activity. The decision package identifies goals and objectives, describes the consequences of not performing the activity, outlines measures of performance, gives alternative courses of action, plus costs and benefits of both requested and alternative activities. Armed with these data, management can evaluate and rank each activity and then decide whether to allocate funds for the service.

Decision packages for the information needs of an organization should include the following: managing the information facility, generating the information base, maintaining the information or data base, developing and organizing the information or data base, establishing reference and referral services, maintaining automated services, and consulting outside services such as information brokers.

While there are many methods of constructing a budget, such as zero base budgeting and the planning-programming-budgeting system, there are basically five different types of budgets:

1. The line-item budget—the most common type—is, as its name implies, constructed around a series of lines, each one representing a different item of expense. There may be a line for compensation, another for facilities, one for materials and supplies, and so on. The breakdown may be very detailed, with an item such as compensation being broken down into salaries for professionals, nonprofessionals, consultants, and clerical help. One reason the line-item budget is popular is that you can locate a specific item in the budget and compare it with every other item.
2. The lump-sum budget is also self-descriptive. The organization allocates a certain amount of money to operate its information center. The information manager then decides how to divide the sum among various requirements. The manager may decide to forgo the purchase of new equipment or terminate a service already in effect to stay within budget limitations. Thus, although the amount of money is handled as a lump sum by higher echelons of management, it is eventually translated into actual line items for disbursement.
3. In a formula budget, allocation for one department is determined by the performance of other functions in the organization. For example, in one company the information center receives 1 percent of sales. In other companies, allocation is based on a percentage of research and development funding. The formula budget is similar to the lump-sum budget in that it merely deter-

mines how much money the information center gets, not how the department spends the money.

4. The performance budget is based on what the information center does and the level of services it is expected to deliver. The performance budget requires that the information manager develop a unit cost for each product or service rendered. The unit cost is determined by dividing the total cost of producing a number of units of work by the number of units produced. For example, if last year's cost for off-line printouts of citations was $300, and you ordered 2,000 printouts, the unit cost for off-line printing would be 15¢ ($300 divided by 2,000). Similarly, to obtain labor costs for each productive hour you must add the basic salary cost to payments for sick leave, tuition subsidies, vacations, and so on, and divide by the number of hours actually used in productive work. The eight-hour work day may really shrink to a six-hour day devoted to productive work. The information center's budget is based on the volume of activities expected for the year times the unit cost for the various activities.

5. Program budgeting allocates funding for the organization's various programs. For example, the manager of each program or function is given a specified amount of money to be used for information services. Certain programs are more information-intensive than others, and so more money will be apportioned to them for information support than to others. Research and development programs as well as the marketing function are notably high information users.

Budgeting an Information Center

Regardless of the type of budget or the method of budget construction, the information center must maintain a principle of truth in spending. This is accomplished by knowing and controlling direct expenses, direct labor, and indirect charges. Since each industry has unique information demands and companies within an industry have varying needs for information and information services, it is more practical to deal with guidelines rather than actual dollar allocations.

In planning your budget you must assess start-up costs, annual operating expenses, and future needs. First consider the actual physical space. Initial costs of constructing, purchasing, or renting a facility are high. Be sure to allow for a five-year growth pattern. The initial expenditure is basically a nonrecurring cost, but do allocate money each year for renovations that may be necessary. Space to house technological improvements that are on the drawing board today should go into your budget plans, marked for future expansion or possibly a new location.

Equipment and furnishings are also expensive initially. Costs of reading tables and chairs for users, copying machines, microform readers and printers, audio cassette players, videotape players, computer terminals linked to printers, and tape cassette recorders and players must be considered. The traditional stacks for books and periodicals and work tables for the staff must be added into the equipment budget. There is also off-site equipment that is linked to your main facility. Facsimile equipment, computer terminals, telecommunication requirements, and word processing machines are but a few of the items. Each year you will have to set aside funds for repairs, replacements, and additional equipment as needed. New technology is a mainstay of the information industry and these future needs should be noted in your five-year projections.

Salaries and wages will constitute approximately 70 percent of your budget. You may want to include funds for the services of an information consultant as well as those for the professional, nonprofessional, and clerical labor that will become part of your annual operating budget. Merit increases, promotions, and additional staff requirements will also have to be taken into account.

Approximately 25 percent of your budget will be devoted to establishing your basic information collection. This information resource may consist of books, journals, proceedings, market research reports, microforms, audiovisual material, data bases, and so on. After your initial outlay, you will have to budget money for subscriptions, for updating your basic reference collection, and for on-line services. When determining the cost for on-line services, be sure to consider all direct costs: computer time, telecommunications connect time, off-line printing, and labor charges for your searchers. Future needs will be determined by new fields of interest of your organization, and so you must project the cost of extending your collection to meet these needs.

Expenditures of materials and supplies will be high the first year; for subsequent years, figure on an annual operating expenditure of about 3 percent of your total budget for these expendables. In addition to the standard office supplies, special paper is needed for the printer attached to the computer terminal and special supplies and paper are needed for copying machines and microform printers. Be sure to include contingency budgets for unusual requirements.

Finally, allocate about 2 percent of your budget for such important miscellaneous items as travel, membership dues, training, and promotion. For example, each of the major vendors of on-line services provides beginning and advance training classes in the various data bases they offer. As new data bases appear on the market and old data bases are reprogrammed to include additional features, it is imperative that your staff members attend periodic training sessions. These training sessions may be held at the vendor's facility (in major cities throughout the United States and abroad), at the professional meetings, or at your own site. The manager of the information center must set aside funds for promotion of the information itself. Unless you alert your potential users to what you can offer them and let those already using your services know what new services you can provide, your information resources will remain unused. The only value information has is when it is put to use.

AUDITING

As a manager in the private, public, or nonprofit sector, your responsibility is to measure and evaluate your information products and services to be sure you are getting the maximum return from your financial commitment for information. You fulfill this management obligation by conducting an information audit—a methodical examination and review of your information assets.

Essentially, the information audit is a comprehensive operational audit that seeks to answer the following types of questions: Does the company have the information resources needed to achieve its organizational objectives? Are the information assets accurate and current? Are the information assets and information-related equipment and materials used efficiently? Do the information personnel operate effectively in providing all levels of management with information in the medium and format that will offer the maximum impact for decision making? Where are problem areas that, if corrected, will result in better operations and increased profits for the company?

You can conduct a broad, confidential questionnaire survey, interview selected members of the organization, record critical incidents where good or bad information affected the outcome of company goals, maintain information diaries over a three- or five-day period, or prepare an analysis of information flow. Depending on the circumstances and the desired depth of the audit, you may use any or all of these or other techniques.

The information audit is not only helpful in addressing known problems dealing with information, but aids in identifying potential trouble spots that could cause serious problems in the future. The information audit can serve as an "early warning system" to identify those information resources that should be obtained now so they will be available to the organization when they are needed in the future.

You must conduct an inventory of information resources. Resources include both the internally and externally generated documents you have in your organization, in whatever medium they may exist. The inventory must include the holdings of the technical information center, company library, marketing data center, components information center, data processing tape library, specifications file, records center, and so on. Evidence of overlap, duplication, and proliferation of facilities and services are indicative of what an information audit may uncover.

Once these information elements are accounted for, they must be evaluated for accuracy and relevance to your company's current and long-range aims. Collecting information just to impress management with statistical data is deceptive and deceitful. For example, one information audit disclosed that a company maintained complete studies on airport systems—five years after it decided to discontinue its activities in this field. As a matter of fact, another division of the corporation, 2,000 miles away, had taken on this area of work as part of its charter and had developed its own information resources independent of the previous group. The five-year-old material was riot accurate in light of new government regulations and was irrelevant to the needs of that particular division. The removal of unneeded information from active files is an area of concern for information auditing.

Simply having information available is not enough. An audit should reveal if the information can be retrieved when required, and how quickly. An inventory card may indicate that you have a particular piece of information, but that won't help the manager who needs the report if it has been misfiled, lost, or stolen. The recall ratio is the number of potentially relevant items retrieved out of the total number of relevant items summoned from the collection. This quantitative measure does not take into account the amount of information recalled erroneously. Thus the auditor must also apply a relevance or precision ratio, which measures how many of the recalled items are germane to the material needed. The relevance ratio is the number of pertinent documents that are sorted out of the number of documents retrieved. There is an inverse relationship between the recall and relevance ratios. The more information produced, the less its relevance to the question at hand. The recall ratio is a quantitative measure and the relevance ratio is a qualitative one.

Some relevant items may be located in an information data base in a few minutes, but take four weeks to acquire. That is another type of problem that an information audit spotlights.

Simplicity and flexibility in information systems are other areas that come within the information audit's scope. In-house systems that are incompatible with other systems are not cost-effective. The information audit will let you know if a method of retrieving information requires extensive training and demands operation by highly technical personnel.

User orientation is also a prime concern of the information audit. The accessibility of the information, the physical location, and the information-related hardware must be audited. The easier it is for the ultimate user to obtain information, the more cost-effective the operation is. Does the user always have to go to an information center to obtain material, or can data be sent or phoned to the user's office? Is the information immediately usable, or must the material be rearranged? Are the hours of operation dictated by the users' convenience or the pleasure of the information staff? Does the user find the information useful? These are but a few of the questions that an information audit must ask.

Also, the organizational structure of the information center must be audited. Is it compatible with the way the rest of the organization is structured? What is the ratio of professional staff to nonprofessional members and clerical staff? Does the information manager have sufficient status to attend upper-level staff meetings to learn what the current and future needs of the company are? For example, in one company the information audit showed that copies of company-sensitive information, such as the five-year plan, were not housed in the information center for controlled distribution and that the information manager was not allowed to see a copy of the document! The stated goals of the company were denied to a group whose responsibility was to produce information to support those goals.

The costs and benefits of information are also proper areas of concern of the information audit. How much, if anything, a user is willing to pay for information products and services is the acid test of how important information is in his management duties. It is also a good indicator as to how effective, efficient, and beneficial the information center is in its operations. Information cost recovery may range from charges for on-line searches to fees for quick responses to reference questions, reproduction costs, charges for documents, and translations, costs incurred through use of information brokers, costs in acquiring, processing, and maintaining information products, and so on.

The information audit reveals the extent to which the information products and services have value, benefit, and use for the company. If the information center scores high in these areas then it is meeting its goals, which are in line with the organization's overall goals. Areas that need corrective action to improve effectiveness and efficiency can be implemented and information gaps can be filled once they are noted.

Should the information audit be conducted by internal auditors or by independent public accountants? It is not an either/or situation; both internal auditors and independent public accountants should conduct information compilations, reviews, and full-scale audits. Today companies are required to state fairly their financial positions, in accordance with accepted accounting principles. With information now being recognized as a major corporate resource, the same type of disclosure of the information assets will someday be an integral part of the financial statement. For example, Arthur D. Little, Inc., has already registered the term "The Information Audit" as a service trademark of its management consulting firm.

Planning, budgeting, and auditing information resources are responsibilities that upper-level management must be cognizant of and implement. These mechanisms require you to assess your information needs to achieve your company's long-term goals through information-based decisions and strategies.

REFERENCES

1. Forest Woody Horton, Jr., "Budgeting and Accounting for Information," *The Government Accountant's Journal*, Vol. 28, No. 1 (Spring 1979), p. 31.
2. John F. Rockart, "Chief Executives Define Their Own Data Needs," *Harvard Business Review*, March–April 1979, pp. 81–93.
3. *Public Papers of the Presidents of the United States: Lyndon Baines Johnson*, August 25, 1965 (Book II, Item No. 447), p. 917.

7

MANAGING THE LIFE CYCLE
OF INFORMATION

Four key resources have to be managed consistently, sys-
tematically, and conscientiously for productivity. They are
capital, crucial physical assets, time, and knowledge. Each
of these resources has to be managed separately and dif-
ferently.[1]

—Peter F. Drucker

Information: Plan it, budget it, audit it. Above all, *manage* it.

The information manager has prime responsibility for managing
the various phases of the information life cycle, but every manager
in the organization is involved. All managers provide and use information. And you as a manager must take an active part in over-
seeing its life cycle: its generation, reproduction and distribution,
acquisition, processing, retention, and assimilation.

GENERATING INFORMATION

As the Age of Information becomes a reality, the "product" that
results from research and development is likely to be information,
not hardware. Information may be generated as a normal written
report, an oral presentation, a graphic display, or a hybrid of several
of the above that results in a multimedia communication.

You must organize and plan a work environment that engenders
the creation of information. This is not to imply that your organization should contribute to the paperwork problem that is already stifling the creative process in many companies. Rather, you should

91

encourage the flow of new information from within your organization by nurturing and developing the information your employees
are already providing and by spotting areas in which more information is needed to meet the corporation's long- and short-range
goals.

Today, the effective manager must recruit and retain information-oriented personnel. He must be versatile in organizing programs and tasks in a way that promotes new ideas and must be dynamic in encouraging his team to excel in its assignments. The
effective manager is people oriented in the midst of the high technology that symbolizes the Age of Information.

To create an organizational climate that is hospitable to information generation, you as a manager must not only be finely tuned
to the organization's goals and well informed about the requirements of your own responsibilities—you must also be able to ask
the smart questions that stimulate thought processes in your employees.

Before hiring personnel you must know what skills you need.
Having established these criteria you will be better able to recognize
the talents needed in the people you interview for positions. Ask
yourself: Does the potential employee appear to be professionally
competent? Are there indications he or she learns quickly? What
innovative approaches has the person taken to meet challenges?
What does the prospect's resume show regarding continuous self-
development? In conversation does the individual display an attitude of self-motivation? Does the person demonstrate intellectual
curiosity and initiative? Maturity? Can the person operate with
minimum supervision? Will the prospective new employee function
well under stress? The work may demand a high degree of team-
work—how well will the person work with others?

To staff an operation high in information output, you may be
hiring people who have more talent than you do in certain areas.
(Unfortunately, too often an organization is staffed with mediocre
people because the manager feels threatened by people who may be
more competent than he is in certain specialties.) You yourself must
develop and demonstrate a sense of self-confidence, based on your

overall knowledge and managerial skills. This is the only way to channel the energies of these highly capable information workers in a positive mode.

Once your organization is staffed, you must establish an environment that will support these individuals in developing new ideas. The typical pyramid organization chart that shows the information giver at the top directing lower-level operations is not descriptive of an organization that is responsive to the demands of information generation. A flat or horizontal management structure is flexible, allowing individuals and specialized departments to more easily inform management of new opportunities, ideas, and concepts. But an information-responsive climate goes beyond the geometric representation of the organization. It means you must insert yourself into the organization as someone who integrates information—a catalytic agent that stimulates thinking, a synergistic force that coalesces diverse information elements. The result is greater information benefits.

The managers of groups in which information is generated can expect to encounter areas of conflict among the individuals within the organization. To maintain the steady flow of information from your organization, these conflicts must be resolved—not repressed. Bring conflicting ideas to the surface in an open, information-supportive forum. Encourage competitive ideas. Inform, don't provoke. Many seemingly irreconcilable differences can be merged into a unifying concept that encompasses several ideas. Together, those ideas can make a strong approach to solving a problem. Educate your employees about the inherent worth of all information. (Although some information cannot be applied immediately, it might be the key element in attaining a company objective at another time.) There must be a feeling that the organization respects the efforts of all employees to generate and use information.

Be aware of those elements that promote the development of information. Allow your employees easy access to supportive areas such as typing assistance, computer time, and especially information facilities like libraries and information centers. However, be aware that making these and similar aids available will not automatically stimulate information output. As a matter of fact, if they are not handled properly, these services may actually hinder output. The internal red tape of filling out request forms for services, having the forms approved, and dealing with delays is frustrating and can have a deleterious effect on your staff of knowledge workers.

You, as a manager, must make sure these services are available to your personnel. It's not uncommon for people to spend more time getting permission than they spend generating information. If this is the case your staff will avoid these service areas and associated bottlenecks and try to get help by other means. The bottom line: less productivity, increased frustration and anger, and the eventual stifling of information generation.

Your personal involvement and encouragement are critical to the effective operation of your technical services to support your personnel. Involvement means taking an interest in what your people are doing—it does not mean replacing weekly progress reports with interrogations. Once you establish standards of professional performance and clearly delineate organizational objectives, your involvement is to reward (psychologically and monetarily) those who achieve, and to help those employees who need assistance. The manager who seeks to create a climate of high information output has the responsibility of shielding his subordinates from many of the administrative chores that are held over from the Industrial Age. Control is necessary, but it must not inhibit information flow. Control must be flexible enough to channel growth to meet objectives.

REPRODUCING AND DISTRIBUTING INFORMATION

After information has been generated it must be reproduced and distributed to other people, who evaluate it, synthesize it, and use it to solve problems, help make timely decisions, or project future opportunities (or risks). Although the information manager or someone else in your organization will be designated to determine the most cost-effective method of reproduction and physical distribution, you as a manager carry the responsibility of making sure your ideas are circulated to the appropriate people (inside and outside your organization) at the appropriate time in a usable form and style.

Information may be reproduced in an oral, written, or audiovisual form. The contents may be verbatim, condensed, or summarized. Media may be face-to-face communication, telephone conversations, printed copies, microforms, audio cassettes, videotapes, computer tab runs, computer output microfilm, facsimile transmission, and so on—whatever equipment your organization has available to receive and transmit information. Businesses have traditionally made few capital investments in communication technology for the office. Ironically, capital investment appears to be a lagging indicator of economic activity in information technology. For example, the farm worker in the United States has a capital investment of about $75,000 but the factory worker only approximately half that amount. Compare this with the office worker with only about $2,000 worth of capital equipment supporting him. Most managers in today's information-oriented world of work do not have much communications technology available to them.

Although you may lack technology, you can and must have a mind-set that recognizes the importance of information distribution. You need to inform your own people of the company's objectives and goals, and you must also be receptive to the information your employees have to offer. Studies show a 10 percent information loss accrues from the board of directors to the president. By the time it filters to the vice president, approximately 65 percent of the initial information is intact. The managers or directors end up with 50 percent of the information, first-line supervisors with 30 percent, and nonmanagement members with 20 percent of the board of directors' information. If an 80 percent loss of information seems deplorable (of course some is intentional), think how difficult it is for your employees to transmit their information upward to higher levels of management.

Disasters have occurred because of poor exchange of information within an organization. A French Senate committee investigated the delays in containing 65 million gallons of crude oil that polluted the coast of France when the supertanker Amoco Cadiz broke up off the coast of Brittany in March 1978. The report showed that at least six government agencies were involved. The delays were caused by lack of coordination resulting from poor information distribution. The report stated that:

> ... information is divided among some agencies which are unaware of each other, more or less, or the information is in some ways broken down into pieces and poorly distributed, or finally and paradoxically the agency which has the competence to intervene does not know about the information. At times it is a system lacking in orderly continuity, but it is always marked by a pretended coordination replacing the unity of command which is essential to confront the danger, at first potential then real. The agency which has the power has not the means, those who have the means do not have the powers, and those who have the information have neither.[2]

Authority, power, and information are the three essentials needed for a manager to function effectively and efficiently. The black tide that brought economic disaster to the coast of Brittany is a striking example of what can occur when an organization, private or public, is hamstrung through lack of information, authority, or power to act on that information.

The Three Mile Island incident in the United States is another disastrous example of poor information distribution specifically, and nonmanagement of the information life cycle generally. The President's commission investigating the accident concluded that the Nuclear Regulatory Commission, responsible for licensing and regulating commercial reactors; Metropolitan Edison Company, operator and part owner of the Three Mile Island nuclear power plant; Babcock & Wilcox, designer and supplier of the reactor and nuclear steam supply system; and General Public Utilities Corporation, a utilities holding company that is the parent corporation of the three companies that own Three Mile Island, are all information-deficient. The following excerpts from the 1979 *Report of the President's Commission on the Accident at Three Mile Island* are official testimony to the potential dangers that lurk in any business, industry, and government agency when management neglects the important need for information.

1. The response to the emergency was dominated by an atmosphere of almost total confusion. There was a lack of communication at all levels. Many key recommendations were made by individuals who were not in possession of accurate information, and those who managed the accident were slow to realize the significance of the events that had taken place.[3]

2. There is little evidence of the impact of modern information technology within the control room.[4]

3. Information was not presented in a clear and sufficiently understandable form.[5]

4. The major offices within the NRC operate independently with little evidence of exchange of information or experience.[6]

5. In a number of important cases, General Public Utilities Corporation (GPU), Met Ed, and B&W failed to acquire enough information about safety problems, failed to analyze adequately what information they did acquire, or failed to act on that information. Thus, there were a serious lack of communication about several critical safety matters within and among the companies involved in the building and operation of the TMI-2 plant.[7]

As these dramatic events indicate, management effectiveness is directly related to how well all aspects of the life cycle of information are managed. Failure to recognize the importance of information as a manageable resource in every element of an organization may have effects that transcend the loss of profits and the decline in your company's share of the market—it may even result in disasters and possible deaths.

ACQUIRING INFORMATION

Every manager in your organization should be responsible for keeping his or her eyes and ears open to the facts and forecasts relating to your company's operations. Your business, professional, and social contacts provide informal but highly effective ways of gathering information.

Using modern technology, today's manager has access to millions of items that have been published or recorded in various media. Here your information manager and his staff can be of great help to you. But an equally valuable information resource exists. It is unwritten, unrecorded, but essential for your organization's well-being.

For example, during an informal talk with a state representative one business manager was alerted to the fact that legislation was being drawn up that would significantly impact the company's distribution of goods. He reported the details of his conversation to his company's executives. The information center manager was asked to find out if similar bills had been enacted in other states and what their effects were on businesses like theirs. Armed with this information, the company president traveled to the state capital, explained the deleterious effects that would occur if the legislation were enacted, and suggested two alternative pieces of legislation that could benefit both the state and the business. The bottom line was that a bill was finally passed that considered the interests of both the company and the state.

Another example occurred not in the political arena, but in the field of technology. At a scientific conclave two engineers met at a display booth in the exhibition hall. In passing, the first one mentioned to the second that the product being demonstrated was of interest to his company but did not quite meet its needs. He spelled out his company's technical requirements and his quick-minded colleague said he was sure that his company had the exact product that was required. They exchanged business cards and the second engineer phoned his home office. Before the conference was over, his marketing department manager sent a salesman and an engineer to discuss the project with the potential customer. The result: a contract to supply the needed hardware. The second engineer had gone to the conference with the basic intention of acquiring technical information, but in the process picked up marketing information that was beneficial to the company as a whole.

Employees must be trained to scan both internal and external environments for information with potential value to your organization. Your personnel must be aware of all your product lines and services, not just the ones they work on. It is vital that they understand the company's goals and objectives, know what new ventures are planned, and are informed about activities that are scheduled to be phased out. (Just as money begets money, information begets needed information.)

The saddest comment one hears from a business executive is: "If I had only known." Because it need not be. In many cases there are people in the organization who have knowledge of a situation or event, but are unaware of its potential impact on the corporate body and so do not supply management with vital data.

One method of overcoming the apathy toward information acquisition is to have employees prepare an "information report" after each company trip. This does not take the place of a detailed trip report. The information report is a simple form in which every department is listed and the reporter jots down any information that may be of interest to those departments. The report is sent to the information center where the information contained in it is evaluated quickly and the appropriate departments are notified. If no information has been acquired the employee states this in his information report.

The information report is also a useful tool for motivating employees to provide items they come across in their own personal endeavors. The person who files the first report of information that turns out to be relevant and upon which the company takes action is rewarded financially. All information reports are forwarded to the information center, which acts as a clearinghouse in screening and forwarding the material and in following up if any actions were taken. (One individual had spoken with his stockbroker, who mentioned that he had just talked with an employee at a New York bank and had received the impression that the prime rate was going to be raised in two days. He reported the gist of the conversation on an information report and turned it into the information center. The information was relayed to the finance director and a major capital investment that had been pending was approved for immediate purchase.)

Some managers feel that such surreptitious acquisition of information feeds the rumor mill and that most information acquired in this manner is irrelevant and time consuming. The grapevine will always exist. The key is to tap the grapevine for information that may prove profitable for the company. Actually, uncovering false rumors is an important concern of all managers. By bringing these tales and rumors into the open, the manager can counteract them with honest answers. As long as half-truths persist the workforce will be demoralized, which results in lower productivity and higher anxiety levels. Thus management must be continually alert to all types of information that may affect not only new business opportunities, technological breakthroughs, and competitive risks, but also those items that are of concern to the men and women who make up the organization.

Information acquisition can be broken down into three general methods. First, scanning. This means keeping tuned to political, social, economic, and technological activities that may have an immediate or long-range effect on your organization. Second, monitoring. Here you focus on activities that need to be watched constantly for changes that may have an impact on your company. Third, tracking. In this category, the information is so critical that it is continuously gathered, synthesized, and evaluated. At least two information data base producers offer tracking services: The Information Bank (New York Times Company) and Disclosure, Inc. The latter organization will automatically send you copies of all reports filed with the Securities and Exchange Commission on companies you have designated to be tracked. Key Issues Tracking System is the name given by The Information Bank to its service that provides daily updates on fast-changing events.

PROCESSING INFORMATION

Data processing and word processing are common terms in most business operations today. Information processing is now part of the business vocabulary. But information processing is much more than cataloging, classifying, indexing, and abstracting information for later identification and location. You, the manager, must eventually process this information mentally for decision making and planning.

According to Henry Mintzberg, associate professor in the Faculty of Management at McGill University, Montreal, Canada:

The processing of information is a key part of the manager's job. In my study, the chief executives spent 40% of their contact time on activities devoted exclusively to the transmission of information; 70% of their incoming mail was purely informational (as opposed to requests for action). The manager does not leave meetings or hang up the telephone in order to get back to work. In large part, communication *is* his work.[8]

The first step in processing information at the managerial level is evaluating the information for completeness. Too often the information provided is subjective, not objective. It is the result of single-factor analysis that produces tendentious information that will benefit a single person or department. But what about opposing views? Alternatives? Disadvantages? These and similar pragmatic questions will force you to evaluate the complete issue. Completeness does not imply that you will know everything about anything. What it does mean is that you are reasonably certain no major elements are missing from the information.

After you have established that the information is complete in scope and depth you must determine its accuracy. Reporters require at least two sources for the same information. Similarly, information managers verify "soft" information from more than one source. In a business organization it is vital that you have more than official channels of information open to you. Once your staff becomes aware that you do check information for accuracy, they will be careful to provide you with valid information.

The third step in information processing is linkage. This is the judgmental factor that determines how the information affects your current operations and future plans. As Carll Tucker, editor of *Saturday Review,* writes, "Disembodied facts are fool's gold. They are so easy to mistake for true learning. But only the connections between facts can show us how the world works."[9] The most mentally demanding job a manager has is to decide what opportunities and risks for the company will result from applying the information at hand. All sorts of econometric models and regression analysis methods purport to answer the "what-if" questions that plague you. But in the end, you, the manager, must decide what the implications of the information are. You must process that information, based on your years of experience and your expert knowledge of your own company and the industry within which it operates. You understand the competitive forces that affect your organization. And remember; as new information becomes available you may need to alter your decisions.

RETAINING INFORMATION

The government has a major impact on business organizations' retention of information. Various government agencies mandate what records must be retained and for how long. Each year the *Federal Register* publishes a "Guide to Record Retention Requirements," which contains more than 1,000 digests of the federal regulations that specify required retention periods for records. Your information manager can supply you with this information. He can also recommend the best methods of storing information and specify the appropriate form of storage (original copies, microforms, or computerized systems).

Some personal information packages are not governed by federal decree. You must determine how best to store and retrieve certain information for your own use. According to the Mintzberg study mentioned earlier, most managers seek out information, not through computers or written memos, but by word of mouth. This presents a problem, because on average, people remember only half of what they have just heard. After two months they recall only about 25 percent of the conversation.[10]

A 75 percent loss of information in 60 days is too high a figure for a manager to sustain in the Age of Information. You must record the essence of oral communications in some way. Your aide-memoire may take the form of a written memo, dictation into an audio cassette, or input to a computer. Whatever the form, the information must be dated, given a subject, and assigned a date for destruction (or a date for reevaluating whether or not it should be retained).

This does not mean you will need to establish a warehouse of personal information. Your information retention program will usually result in about 25 percent of your recorded information being retained in an active file, 15 percent in inactive, and 60 percent destroyed. The National Records Management Council, Inc., states that only about 5 percent of information filed is ever reused after one year.

Systematically managing your private files will provide you with an information base from which you can make informed decisions, more accurate forecasts, and sounder plans.

ASSIMILATING INFORMATION

Management throughout the organization is also involved in the last phase of the information cycle, information assimilation: the internalization and utilization of information. However, many times new information results in changes, and it is a psychological axiom that people resist change.

Even in highly information-dependent organizations it is difficult for both management and nonmanagement personnel to accept information that conflicts with their current mode of operations and planning or that requires procedural changes. Resistance may not take the form of outright rejection but will appear in more subtle ways. One method involves excessive requests for more information on a subject. Accrual of information leading to knowledge or proficiency can be described by a J curve. Let's assume you start out knowing little or nothing about the subject. As you acquire more information, you realize how little you actually know about the area being researched. Some of the material you thought was valid may prove to be invalid. Thus for a short period in the beginning of your research you may have less real information than you started with. Soon, however, you'll come upon the needed information—you've hit the bottom of the J curve and your knowledge will increase as more and more information becomes available. Those who resist acting upon the newly acquired information insist that additional information must be sought out before decisions can be made and actions taken. This delay in accepting, assimilating, and using the information can be detrimental to the company. In physics, the Heisenberg uncertainty principle describes the limits of what is knowable in quantum mechanics. In information science, there is an indeterminacy principle too: Beyond a certain point the information and all its ramifications cannot be measured. In that realm, experience and management judgment take over for final decisions. When the information validates and reinforces previous decisions and actions there is no problem; the proof, evidence, and support that management has acted wisely exist. But when information creates questions or negates prior actions or proposed efforts, human defense mechanisms come into play. Managers challenge, deny, and manipulate information to suit the needs of those responsible for the previous decisions or the projected plans.

Another hindrance to information assimilation comes from those who have the information but refuse to admit it. They deny their knowledge with such expressions as, "Well, no one ever told me," or "I didn't know that," or "I don't understand." The truth is they do understand, but do not agree with information that challenges their predispositions.

You, as a manager, must establish a climate for information assimilation. It is imperative that you encourage and stimulate an environment that is hospitable to positive, negative, or neutral information that deals with your organization. It is this final phase of information assimilation that regenerates the life cycle of information. A regenerative process can occur only where information is not considered a threat, but a needed and vital asset to the company. Information must be assimilated and put to use just like capital and labor. As a manager you must assume the responsibility of becoming an information determinist—a person who realizes that information shapes your own and your organization's destiny, and that information can be managed.

REFERENCES

1. Peter F. Drucker, *Managing in Turbulent Times* (New York: Harper & Row, 1980), p. 20.
2. Rapport No. 486, Sénat, Seconds Session Ordinaire de 1977–1978, Paris, France, 29 Juin 1978, p. 223.
3. *Report of the President's Commission on the Accident at Three Mile Island,* Washington, D.C., October 1979, p. 17.
4. *Ibid.,* p. 11.

5. *Ibid.*
6. *Ibid.*, p. 52.
7. *Ibid.*, p. 43.
8. Henry Mintzberg, "The Manager's Job: Folklore and Fact," *Harvard Business Review*, July–August 1975, p. 56.
9. Carll Tucker, "In the Matter of Facts," *Saturday Review*, March 15, 1980, p. 54. Copyright © 1980 by *Saturday Review*. All Rights Reserved. Reprinted with Permission.
10. Ralph G. Nichols and Leonard A. Stevens, *Are You Listening?* (New York: McGraw-Hill, 1957), pp. 5–6.

Part III:
The Information Manager

8

ORGANIZATIONAL STRUCTURE

... the convergence of technologies is placing a great strain on the organization. The new technologies don't fit in the old organizational boxes. To attain the Office of the Future, we must organize for the future.[1]
—*Fenwicke W. Holmes*

The organizational structure of any company is designed to define and delineate clearly authority and responsibility relationships among the various members of the company, for the attainment of the stated aims and goals of the company. But organizations cannot be structured in a vacuum. You must consider the changes that are occurring in the world about you and how these changes affect your company's declared objectives and the products and services your company produces and markets.

DRIVING FORCES

Two primary driving forces will determine your company's organizational structure in the Age of Information. The first is management's recognition and acceptance of the concept that information is a corporate resource. The second involves the advances in and the convergence of information technologies that affect every operation in your organization. Top-level management must finally accept the fact that information (and its related information services) is not solely a support function. You buy, trade, and sell information in today's marketplace. Given the economic realities of today's business environment, you must adopt a holistic view of the need and uses for information if you are to compete, prosper, and grow.

Other trends will force you to reappraise your organizational structure. The role of governments, and their demands for more and more information, affect every company in the world. In the United States in 1979, small businesses alone spent $12.7 billion filling out government forms. An *INC.* magazine study of 1,000 businesses showed that 7.3 billion questions on 305 million forms were answered in 1979. Yet there is another side of government policies, one which encourages the growth of unregulated industries. When the Federal Communications Commission deregulated the marketing of terminal equipment for the telecommunications industry in April 1980, FCC chairman Charles D. Ferris said, "Today we have removed the barricades from the door to the Information Age. Government will no longer be a barrier that prevents or delays the introduction of innovations in technology."[2]

Even as lifestyles are shifting at an accelerated pace, markets are changing too. Companies must respond to consumer needs as the economy changes in every sector and social stratum throughout the United States. Information about the cultural, social, and economic aspects of various geographic areas becomes increasingly critical in business as corporations reorganize to sell products and services on a regional basis. Added to this is the emergence of worldwide markets, which put even greater demands on managers for information about consumer needs overseas.

Raw materials and energy are increasing in costs, decreasing in supply. Information will play a vital role in the management of these resources to assure a steady supply of materials and efficient use of traditional energy sources and to help us move toward the discovery of alternative methods to our oil dependency.

EMERGENCE OF THE INFORMATION DEPARTMENT

There's nothing new about the need for information in business, industry, and government. As various information technologies and disciplines are developed they have been incorporated into business organizations as service groups. Data processing has been rapidly assimilated into the business world. Historically, this service group was usually assigned first to the comptroller's office, where it was used primarily to process financial data. As software has become more sophisticated and more uses of data processing equipment have been added, the data processing department has become a separate, centralized entity serving all the data processing needs of the company.

Similarly, when word processing entered the business scene it was viewed as a support function, usually being placed under the management supervision of the venturesome project or group that was daring enough to adopt the technology. As the advantages of word processing became known and news of its versatility spread throughout the company, it was centralized, becoming part of the administrative services division.

The mail room service, distributing the company mail both internally and externally, is another function of information handling. With time it has become mechanized and automated. Usually it, too, is considered a part of the administrative or office services.

Telecommunications started out as a switchboard service. Then it expanded to include new telephone technology such as the private branch exchange (PBX), private internal telephone (PAX), and Centrex, with its feature of direct inward dialing. The telegram and cablegram needs of a company have usually been put under the control of the telecommunications department. Such services as Telex/TWX and facsimile transmission have found their place, along with the telephone, under the control of one department.

The ubiquitous copying machines are now standard equipment in even the smallest organizations. Originally they were usually under the control of the already existing reprographics or print shop departments of larger companies. Micrographics and computer output microforms originally started out as separate service units in an organization. However, many companies now merge micrographics and reprographics in one centralized department.

The company library developed from the part-time functions of acquiring, storing, and retrieving external and internal information in books, reports, and journals into the full-time professional discipline now called a special library. As management's needs for timely, accurate information have increased, the special library has emerged as an information center with on-line services and analysis, synthesis, and evaluation of information. Other service groups have dealt with the processing of data; the information center has actually researched information for management decisions and problem solving.

Audiovisual departments have come into their own in larger companies where they are responsible for preparing visual aids such as overhead transparencies, flip charts, and other graphic material. Merger of the still photography department, cinematography group, and videotape producers is now standard operating practice in those organizations that use these services.

In companies in which heavy emphasis is placed on writing reports and proposals as well as producing manuals and brochures, the editorial services group acts as a support department, serving all elements of the company.

The rapid growth of technology affecting data, voice, image, and text processing demands a new organizational structure for the effective and efficient coordination of these various elements. The alert manager realizes that these diverse groups, which developed independently, serve one ultimate purpose—to process and produce information that will meet the organization's aims and goals.

THE NEW HIERARCHY

Top management must act before the battle lines are drawn in the struggle over who is to be director of the information department. The data processing manager will vie with the word processing manager for total control. The information center manager will argue convincingly that his group—unlike others that deal with data—has always dealt with information. He is already using all the technology to produce the information needs of the organization and so can claim rights to the new position. In many companies administrative department heads are already competing with telecommunications managers for the top slot.

What upper-level managers must consider in resolving this conflict in personal and departmental interests over organizational goals is that it is the resource of information that must be managed. What is needed is an information manager at a level equivalent to the finance director, the personnel director, the manufacturing director, and so on. Specialists with expertise and training in the various disciplines are needed to continue and improve the operations of their highly technical functions. But a manager must coordinate these interrelated, interdependent operations. The information manager may very well come from one of these services or support groups if he or she shows the ability to manage (plan, organize, command, coordinate, and control) information resources as a company asset. The following chapter will deal with the qualities, duties, and responsibilities of the information manager in more detail.

Then what is the ideal information organization?

There is no ideal organization.

Even Peter F. Drucker states, "There is, so far, no clear answer and no satisfactory way to organize information work—though it is clearly a key activity. . . . But as we develop information capacity we will have to grapple with the organizational problem and will have to find answers, or at least approaches."[3]

The optimum—not ideal—information organization will vary from industry to industry and from company to company within each industry because the information demands and needs of every organization differ from each other in kind and degree. But some overriding considerations impinge on all organizations.

Structural Guidelines

Company policy statements must clearly explain that the function of the new hierarchy is to manage the information resources of the organization to attain stated goals and objectives. The policy statements must be so succinct that no one inside or outside the company can misinterpret information management as information manipulation. The concept of information manager must not be tainted with the image of a czar who controls information flow for personal power, status, and authority.

The hotly debated subject of centralization *vs.* decentralization must be resolved. Solutions are hard to come by when the dilemma is stated in a polarized either/or frame of reference. What is needed is centralized control and decentralized authority, with the information manager assuming ultimate responsibility and accountability. With centralized control the information manager formulates policies, determines procedures, and undertakes certain processes. The information manager or director who heads this centralized group assigns staff members to various corporate divisions to service their particular needs. One task force of information scientists is assigned to the engineering division, one or two are located in the marketing division, one group takes care of the information needs of the manufacturing division, and so on. If your company is organized according to various product lines or missions, then an information specialist becomes part of that product or project team and serves its needs and wants in the field of information.

The information manager constantly receives information about the company's information requirements from the staff of people who are on specific assignments. Thus delivery of information is decentralized, while acquisition and processing of information are centralized to avoid duplication, speed up the service, and improve the quality of information being delivered.

The thrust of technology dictates that you must consider alternative institutional arrangements. Information management is not a part of someone else's organization, but is an organizational entity that functions on the same level as the personnel division, the finance division, and the manufacturing division. Information management is no longer separated from the main elements of the company; rather, it is a vital part of the organization.

Another approach is the development of a horizontal rather than a vertical operation. This permits each one of the functional department managers that comprise the information management groups to report directly to the information manager. Thus, with few exceptions, the already existing (but disparate) information-oriented functions remain intact. The resulting change is gradual, slow, and (most importantly) acceptable to the members of the organization. It also emphasizes top management's recognition of these groups, as they now report to a higher level in the overall organization.

A most important point to remember is that there must never be a feeling that empire building is the driving force behind the establishment of an information manager. To the contrary, economies in both scale and organization invariably result in the consolidation and merging of already existing groups, which minimizes the number of people making up the various independent organizations. Grouping together some related functions may also offer the user a one-stop service for information needs.

The span of control by the information manager depends on the extent of the operations of the information division. Since the functions that make up the information division are highly technical, the department heads can each report directly to the information manager. The information manager, with his organizational expertise and managerial ability, will rely on the special technical knowledge of these section heads plus his own awareness of the new technologies that affect each one of these areas. It must be recognized that members of certain groups may resent being incorporated into a new information management division; they may be powerful and influential enough to remain outside the organization. For example, a long-established data processing group may provide services independent of the information management division and yet support the information management group as needed.

Of major concern to the structuring of the information organization is the ultimate information user. The reason for establishing the information management department or division is to provide the users with accurate information when they need it. Too many business managers look at the organizational structure solely from the point of view of efficiency. But what also must be noted is the effectiveness with which the organization meets the demands of its users. The user must be able to make one call or visit to a central organization and state his information needs with the expectation of having the information delivered within a reasonable time. The request may be made by phone, via computer terminal, or in person, depending on the technological sophistication of the organization.

The information may be delivered in the user's choice of media—limited only by the equipment restraints of the company. The information organization must be structured to the user's needs, not the convenience of the information center's staff.

Visibility

An information department organized around a unified structure with centralized control and decentralized authority of all the information resources of your company is not apt to come into being with one masterful stroke of the chart maker's pen. More realistically, it will evolve over a period of time.

It is incumbent upon you as a manager to make the information center viable, flexible, and vital to your company's growth. The information center can become ensconced in a comfortable niche on the organization chart, which will retard its progress. Information center personnel are part of a growth industry, even if the organization or firm with which they are associated has stabilized or is in an economic slump. A commitment to growth must be imparted to the decision makers in the company or government agency to show them how the information center's services can be used to alert managers to opportunities for research, new markets, and technical breakthroughs pertinent to their particular agency. A low profile is usually characteristic of a person low on the totem pole. Your low profile will fall even lower if your department is slashed into nonexistence by cuts in personnel and budget. Don't allow yourself to become too comfortable in your box on the organization chart.

Only one thing is worse than that type of complacency: not having a box in which to be comfortable. Even a one-person information operation should appear on an organization chart. The formal organization chart is a picture of the communication network of your company or bureau. If you're not on the organization chart, you're not part of the information flow in your institution.

An information center must be recognized as an important element in the information flow—to do otherwise is counterproductive. How can you acquire information in anticipation of needs if you are not informed as to what the potential needs are? Your first step must be to position yourself visibly on the organization chart in an area that will afford you the greatest opportunities and options for professional growth.

The position that places you in the mainstream of the communication network of your agency or company, the position that permits you and your department to expand services, the position that offers you the greatest potential for career development, the position that provides the utmost financial and management support—that is the place to be.

Administration Services

In many companies, associations, and government agencies, information personnel are lumped together in a department called administrative services. This department probably also includes the cafeteria, plant security, custodial services, and the mail room. They are sometimes referred to as cost centers.

During economic downturns these support functions are generally the first ones to be cut back, consolidated, or even eliminated. Not because staff members are not providing services efficiently and economically, but because they are viewed as not being directly related to the production and marketing of goods or service, and are therefore not vitally essential.

Being associated with an administrative services group can seriously handicap an information center. First of all, many of the employees that constitute administrative services personnel are primarily nonprofessionals. As a result, the information center manager and his or her staff are considered nonprofessional by association (not by fact). Personal growth and advancement in this type of an organizational situation is at best a desire, seldom an achievement.

Research and Development

Government agencies and private companies that primarily deal in research and development usually place the information center under the research and engineering division. This situation is preferable to being a part of the administrative services division. The scientists and engineers who use the services appreciate the vital role that information plays, and they are generally responsive to requests for additional staffing and increased budgets.

However, if the information center is fortunate enough to be a part of the R&D division, it must be wary of being treated as a support function of that division only. The services it provides, the professional acquisition, processing, and dissemination of information, are really an extension of the research arm of the company. Information center personnel must offer their talents in the same way as professional scientists and engineers. In essence, the information center should strive for a position as a research laboratory because, indeed, it is researching with information. Just as there are optics labs, microprocessing labs, or hydraulic labs in your organization, there should also be an information lab with separate and equal status.

Basic Considerations

Three basic elements must be taken into account when organizing the information department: technology, information, and people.

In many instances the technological factor overshadows the other two aspects because it is highly visible, carries an expensive price tag, and imparts a psychological feeling of sophistication and modernity. Management journals and periodicals accent the importance of technological developments in today's business world and thus perpetuate this single-factor viewpoint. Dramatic concepts of satellite communications systems with earth stations, video display screens, and computerized printouts dominate the thinking of many managers. The successful manager must be cognizant of the importance of information technology in organizing the company's operations, and must also bear in mind that other tools are available. Hardware alone should not determine the organizational arrangement of the business.

Information, the second key element, must be accounted for in shaping the structure of the information center. You must determine the types of information you need for your business to succeed. The spectrum of information is diverse, from financial to scientific, industrial to cultural. But you must also distinguish between the need for data and the need for information. Capturing and processing data for operational requirements is an on-going function in most businesses. What is needed is information based on reliable, accurate data. Information needs vary as the company's objectives and goals change. Every company needs a department that can obtain, process, and deliver the information that management requires at a particular time. Subject specialists in the information department may analyze, synthesize, and evaluate particular types of information needed by all the departments of the company. Coordinating and expediting the flow of information must be given a high priority in designing and building your organizational structure. You need an information gatekeeper who will keep you current on internal and external information that management needs to make the decisions to attain its goals.

People are the most overlooked element in structuring an organization. Yet they are by far the most important. You must not only consider the type of people who will constitute the information department but also the people who will use the information to make decisions about on-going projects, shifts in product lines, development of new processes, and future business. The purpose of information is to help people in the organization meet organizational objectives. People use information so they can accomplish their tasks and expand their capabilities. But it is not always easy to obtain the information you need. When the roadblocks become difficult or numerous, people will seek alternative methods of getting the information—or do without it. It behooves you to develop an organizational structure that will help, not hinder, the men and women of your company in getting the information they need.

Each block on the organization chart contains the names of human beings who have been assigned duties and responsibilities. Too frequently management confuses the organization chart with the organization. The chart merely represents the company. It is not the company itself. The company is people who interact with each other daily to meet company goals. These people do not operate in their boxes on the organization chart; they go about their tasks in the most expeditious ways possible. They obtain, exchange, and evaluate information among each other as the situation demands. Top management must designate one person who will have the authority and responsibility to effectively and efficiently coordinate the information demands of the organization. That person is the information manager.

REFERENCES

1. Fenwicke W. Holmes, "IRM: Organizing for the Office of the Future," *Journal of Systems Management,* 43:1 (January 1979), p. 31.
2. "The FCC Turns Ma Bell Loose," *Newsweek,* April 21, 1980, p. 73. Copyright 1980 by Newsweek, Inc. All Rights Reserved. Reprinted by Permission.
3. Peter F. Drucker, *Management: Tasks, Responsibilities, Practices* (New York: Harper & Row, 1974), p. 539.

9

BECOMING AN INFORMATION MANAGER

*Firms preparing to meet the challenges of the 1980s will
need a capable and sophisticated manager of corporate
information. An organization's success will be dependent
in large part on successfully managing its information resources.* [1]

— *Henry C. Lucas, Jr.*

So you want to be an information manager? You'll have to face and
solve a number of problems. First, how do you apply for a position
that has little official recognition? According to the latest edition of
the Employment and Training Administration's *Dictionary of Occupational Titles* of 20,000 job titles, there is no entry for information manager. And there is no such occupational description in the
Bureau of Labor Statistics' *Occupational Outlook Handbook* for
1980–1981, which covers 274 occupations in detail and briefly men-
tions many other jobs.

The Department of Labor has not yet put the job title of information manager in print; nevertheless, the concept and profession
do exist. Remember, until someone looked down upon the planet
earth from the moon for the first time and witnessed an earthshine,
there was no need for a word to describe that phenomenon. Just as
there were no words like earthshine, astronaut, and cosmonaut at
one time, the vocabulary for the Age of Information is currently
deficient.

But the idea and reality of information management is here. The
cultural time lag between the emergence of a new concept and its

121

general acceptance has delayed the inclusion of the term information manager in the list of job titles in business, industry, and government. This means you have an opportunity to get in on the ground floor of an emerging profession. If you get the proper education and experience and take the right approach, you can sell the idea of information management to your organization. The result is that you can position yourself and your company as innovators and leaders and obtain a competitive edge in the Age of Information.

DEFINITION

The information manager is the individual in an organization (public, private, or nonprofit) who is responsible for acquiring, processing, and using information resources efficiently and for applying those resources effectively to help the organization attain its mission and goals.

To define anything fixes or marks the limits of that which is being defined. The profession of information management is limited only by the initiative, imagination, and industry of the individuals who are willing to meet the challenges of the Age of Information eyeball to eyeball.

Inherent in this broad definition is the requirement that the information manager be familiar with *all* aspects of the information industry, so that the various elements that will best serve the organization's needs are melded. Thus the information manager must have both the education and attitude of a manager, not that of a specialist or technician. He or she is a generalist with the knowledge and skills necessary to plan, organize, and control the information resources of the company. The information manager understands the behavioral aspects of management as well as the technological aspects of information science. Managers and job analysts must keep in mind that tools alone do not define the job. Just being able to handle a T-square and triangle does not make a person an architect. Assuredly one must be familiar with the tools used in a chosen profession. Knowledge of modern techniques of information technology is important for an information manager. But it is only one of the requirements for successfully managing information.

As you embark on a career program in information management—whether you are just entering the world of work or are making a mid-career change—consider the following five points for maximum achievement: self-assessment, career analysis, career plan, career development, and contigency plans.

SELF-ASSESSMENT

Ask yourself these questions: Who am I? What do I prefer? What don't I like? There are many psychological aptitude, attitude, and achievement tests available to you, and many companies and government agencies require you to take such tests. When an organization you want to join administers such quizzes, you'll probably try to second-guess the tests and answer the questions the way you think will get you the job. Don't approach the HIT!² self-assessment test that way.

At this stage you are not applying for a job. You are trying to determine whether or not you want to enter a new field and master the demands of a fast-moving profession. This test will help you decide whether or not you are cut out for this type of work. Remember Polonius' advice to his son: "And this above all: to thine own self be true."

HIT! is a self-assessment test designed to help you determine if you would do well to pursue a career as an information manager. The test is composed of 50 questions, divided into four parts. The first three parts consist of 16 questions each. Part H deals with how you feel about humans, Part I explores your attitude toward information, and Part T investigates your ideas about technology. The fourth part consists of two conceptual questions as to your beliefs about information management.

There are no right or wrong answers. The questions ask you how you feel about certain things. You must choose only one answer for each question. Circle the letter designating your choice. Be candid with yourself. Don't spend time deciding the "correct" answer or diagnosing the question as to what its purpose is. Answer quickly and honestly. No one but you needs to see the results of this test.

SCORING HIT!

This self-assessment test is divided into four parts. The first three parts consist of 16 questions each. Part H deals with how you feel about humans, Part I — your attitude toward information, Part T — your ideas about technology. The fourth part consists of two conceptual questions as to your beliefs about information management.

The scoring system is designed to help you see if your personality matches that of an information manager. There are no correct answers. A high score is no assurance of success, a low score, no indication of failure. The test deals with probabilities, not possibilities.

No.	A	B	C		No.	A	B	C		No.	A	B	C		No.	A	B	C		No.	A	B	C		No.	A	B	C		No.	A	B	C		No.	A	B	C
1.	1	2	1		7.	2	1	1		13.	0	2	1		19.	2	1	1		26.	2	1	1		33.	1	2	2		39.	1	2	2		45.	2	1	1
2.	1	2	1		8.	2	2	1		14.	2	1	2		20.	1	2	2		27.	1	2	0		34.	0	1	2		40.	0	1	2		46.	2	0	2
3.	1	0	2		9.	0	1	2		15.	1	2	0		21.	1	1	2		28.	2	1	1		35.	0	1	0		41.	2	1	0		47.	1	1	2
4.	0	2	1		10.	0	2	0		16.	2	1	0		22.	2	1	2		29.	2	1	2		36.	2	1	1		42.	1	2	1		48.	0	2	1
5.	1	1	2		11.	1	2	1		17.	1	2	1		23.	2	1	0		30.	1	2	2		37.	0	2	1		43.	2	1	0		49.	2	1	1
6.	2	2	0		12.	2	1	1		18.	1	1	2		24.	1	1	2		31.	1	0	2		38.	1	1	2		44.	2	1	2		50.	2	1	1
															25.	2	1	2		32.	0	2	0															

Grade	Assessment
90 and over	You are an information manager.
75 – 89	You have potential to become an information manager.
55 – 74	With more experience, education and attitude changes you may become an information manager.
Below 54	Chances are you would be happier in some profession other than information management.

H

1. I prefer working
   (a) **independently.**
   (b) **as part of a team.**
   (c) **anonymously, like a ghost writer does.**

2. At a party I prefer
   (a) **chatting with old friends.**
   (b) **meeting new people.**
   (c) **having people come over to me to talk.**

3. When I find a new recipe that seems outstanding, I prefer
   (a) **making and serving it, but not giving out the recipe.**
   (b) **letting someone else try it o. t first.**
   (c) **sharing the recipe, even if no one asks for it.**

4. There are times, in a work situation, when I disagree with someone. In such situations I feel it advantageous to
   (a) **get in the last word.**
   (b) **let the other person have his or her say.**
   (c) **keep my mouth shut.**

5. In a controversial issue, I prefer
   (a) **someone to try to influence me to change my line of thinking.**
   (b) **to persuade others to change their attitudes to agree with mine.**
   (c) **to believe there are several ways of looking at an idea.**

6. When a person brings me a personal problem, I
   (a) **try to advise the person what to do.**
   (b) **let the person air the problem, but give no advice.**
   (c) **maintain an impersonal stature and let the person know that home life should be separated from the business world.**

7. Occasionally persons outside of my organization will ask my advice on how best to organize a file of information. I tell them
   (a) **the best way I know how.**
   (b) **they should organize it in a way that is convenient for them.**
   (c) **that as a professional I must charge for giving advice.**

8. When I appraise a person's job performance, I base my evaluations on
   (a) **evidence that can be supported by citing actual events.**
   (b) **overall opinions that others have of the person.**
   (c) **the individual's personality traits.**

9. When I have to give people instructions, I prefer
   (a) **letting them try to find out how to do it by themselves.**
   (b) **preparing written procedures which I distribute to the people.**
   (c) **demonstrating how to do it and then let them try.**

10. In the real world of business and government, developing a backup person or replacement is
    (a) **professional suicide.**
    (b) **a way to allow me to be promoted if such an opportunity occurs.**
    (c) **counterproductive, for a department needs only one boss at a time.**

11. When I have to make a proposal to my boss for additional staff or facilities, I prefer making the proposal
    (a) **in writing.**
    (b) **face-to-face with my boss.**
    (c) **over the telephone.**

12. I find I work best
    (a) **under pressure.**
    (b) **when things are planned and scheduled.**
    (c) **when I'm left alone to develop my own ideas.**

13. Sometimes I have to ask my subordinates for information. When I do I feel
    (a) **embarrassed.**
    (b) **thankful I have a well informed staff.**
    (c) **I must couch the question in a way that will not reveal I don't know the information.**

14. When it comes to developing a budget with my supervisor, I
    (a) **feel it is a subject for negotiation.**
    (b) **give my supervisor my wish list and abide by his or her decision.**
    (c) **will ask my supervisor to review the allocation, if I feel it is insufficient.**

15. When I have to give an oral presentation, I
    (a) **use visual aids to help me remember my speech.**
    (b) **use visual aids to help the audience understand my speech.**
    (c) **avoid using visual aids because they distract from me as the speaker.**

16. When I see the need for change in the system, I
    (a) **take the initiative and proceed in a responsible way.**
    (b) **bring the matter to my supervisor's attention.**
    (c) **feel that in the long run it is best to leave things as they are.**

I

17. I think of information as
    (a) a science.
    (b) an economic resource.
    (c) a way to gain power.
18. In handling information, I prefer
    (a) posting information.
    (b) indexing information.
    (c) classifying information.
19. The successful manager knows how to
    (a) manage information.
    (b) manipulate information.
    (c) filter information.
20. The thing I enjoy most in dealing with information is
    (a) gathering information
    (b) analyzing information.
    (c) synthesizing information.
21. The most reliable information is that which comes from
    (a) a computer.
    (b) government records.
    (c) interviews.
22. I feel that when I give information to a client, I should
    (a) filter out what I think is irrelevant information.
    (b) give the client all the information I have gathered.
    (c) give the minimum amount that is needed for a decision.
23. I feel that a person who wants information in an organization should
    (a) pay for the information service.
    (b) get the information as part of an overhead expense.
    (c) pay only for the amount of information that is found.
24. The type of information I least like to deal with is
    (a) marketing data.
    (b) scientific and technical information.
    (c) personnel records.
25. I believe that an organization should have
    (a) one place to go for information.
    (b) independent marketing information centers, technical information centers, etc.
    (c) centralized acquisition of information but decentralized dissemination.
26. Information centers in business and government should be
    (a) open to all employees.
    (b) available only to professional employees.
    (c) restricted to management personnel.

27. When people ask for information I feel I should
    (a) give them what they ask for.
    (b) ask them why they want the information so as to distinguish between what is wanted and needed.
    (c) demand a need-to-know before revealing the information.
28. I consider information centers in an organization as
    (a) profit centers.
    (b) cost centers.
    (c) power centers.
29. When I don't have access to information a client wants, I
    (a) refer the person to the location of that information.
    (b) tell the client the information is inaccessible.
    (c) give the person a name of an individual who works in that field.
30. I feel decisions should be based on
    (a) information.
    (b) information and intuition.
    (c) information and experience.
31. I have only one reference copy of a report that someone in my organization has prepared. Two people need the report immediately, one for the management section, the other for the technical section.
    (a) I'd lend the report to the person who first asked for it.
    (b) I cannot lend the report because reference copies can't circulate.
    (c) I'd rip the report apart, lending each requestor the needed sections.
32. I feel that one of the qualities of information is that it is
    (a) timeless.
    (b) a management resource.
    (c) overrated in the computer age.

T

33. If I had my choice, I would prefer information in
    (a) books and hard copy reports.
    (b) microfilm and microfiche.
    (c) audio and video cassettes.

34. Computers have their place in the information society, but they
    (a) cause more errors than what they are worth at times.
    (b) are best used for scientific and technical information.
    (c) are best used to process data.

35. Word processing and data processing are not related to information management.
    (a) I agree with this statement.
    (b) I disagree with this statement.
    (c) Only word processing is related to information management.

36. When office equipment fails, I usually first
    (a) try to fix it myself.
    (b) call someone in the office who is handy to fix it.
    (c) call an authorized repairperson.

37. I feel that typing on a computer terminal to retrieve information is
    (a) a clerical job.
    (b) a manager's job.
    (c) a computer or information specialist's job.

38. The reason most companies automate their offices is to
    (a) reduce the number of clerk-typists.
    (b) show their customers they are modern and up to date.
    (c) process information more efficiently.

39. Information technology has put more demands on managers to
    (a) learn how to operate these new machines.
    (b) learn how to best use these machines to aid decision making.
    (c) safeguard information from competitors.

40. I find I get better results when I
    (a) retrieve information manually.
    (b) retrieve information from a computerized data base.
    (c) use both manual and machine methods.

41. Facsimile transmission and so-called electronic mailboxes are
    (a) good in theory and in practice.
    (b) the wave of the future in offices.
    (c) showpieces rather than cost-beneficial equipment.

42. I view the telephone as
    (a) an office nuisance.
    (b) an office aid.
    (c) a necessary office evil.

43. When an office copier needs refilling of paper, I
    (a) do it myself.
    (b) ask one of the staff members to do it.
    (c) leave the machine and wait for the next person to make the refill.

44. When it comes to purchasing equipment for my office, I
    (a) specify exactly what I want.
    (b) tell the purchasing department to make the choice.
    (c) ask one of the other departments to recommend what I should get.

45. When I am operating an office machine and it begins to make unusual sounds and vibrations, the first thing I do is
    (a) pull the plug.
    (b) ask a coworker for aid.
    (c) try to figure out what has gone wrong.

46. I feel that office automation has
    (a) increased productivity.
    (b) demeaned the status of clerical help.
    (c) improved working conditions.

47. I believe that the computerized elements of an information center should come under the supervision of the
    (a) data processing manager.
    (b) word processing manager.
    (c) information manager.

48. Video screens and computer terminals
    (a) dehumanize the office.
    (b) motivate me to try to learn how to use them.
    (c) are for the new hires just coming out of college.

!

49. I feel an information manager deals primarily with
    (a) human beings.
    (b) information.
    (c) technology.

50. I feel the best way to describe an information manager is as
    (a) an entrepreneur.
    (b) a specialist in information.
    (c) an administrator.

CAREER ANALYSIS

After you have determined your own strengths and weaknesses, analyze the career of information management to see if there is a positive match between your aptitudes and interests and what the career demands and has to offer. You may find your desire for the career is greater than your capabilities to become an information manager. Or you may possess all the attributes of a good information manager but find a different career is more attractive to you. Throughout this book you have seen that the job of information manager is a multidimensional career position. You must deal with people: subordinates whom you must manage, peers whose expertise you must coordinate, and superiors whom you must advise as to information needs.

You will be held responsible for the content of the information as well as for handling it. The information has value and cost. Pressures will be put on you to consider the costs *vs.* value in acquiring the best information possible at the least expense within the time and budget constraints of your organization. An information manager must have a working knowledge of economics and finance and an ability to develop and use quantitative data.

An appreciation, awareness, and interest in information technology make up a third dimension of information management. You will be dealing with both established and experimental hardware. You must know the general potentialities and limitations of a variety of equipment that may require high capital expenditures. You will be responsible for recommending or rejecting complex and diversified technology based on your own and your staff's evaluations.

Code of Ethics

All professions are governed by a code of ethics, and this is true of the information profession. If a conflict exists between these ethical commitments and your organization's demands for management of information, you must educate your organization to the paramount importance of ethics in information management. A basic code of ethics encompasses the following items.

- Information managers shall familiarize themselves with all aspects of the information industry so that they may integrate properly the various elements that will best serve their users' needs.
- Information managers shall protect as confidential all information relating to the business, technical, or proprietary operations of their users.
- Information managers shall not accept fees, commissions, or other considerations from, or be affiliated with, those whose supplies, equipment, or services they may specify or recommend to their users.
- Information managers shall provide information to their users that is reliable in context and honest in presentation and shall reveal information whose concealment might mislead their users.
- Information managers shall acquire technical, competitive, and market information for their users only through legal and proper channels.
- Information managers shall serve competing or conflicting users only with the expressed consent of those concerned.
- Information managers shall not intentionally injure the professional reputation, prospects, or business of another information manager.
- Information managers shall conduct themselves in a manner which will enhance the stature of the profession and contribute to the work of information societies, schools with a concern for information management as a profession, and professional publications.

Information management is a career that requires a wide variety of skills, abilities, and personality traits that are physically and mentally demanding, but the results are financially and psychologically rewarding. Unless you can honestly devote yourself to this profession, seek a career in another area.

CAREER PLAN

After you decide to seek a career in information management, you are ready for the next step, which is plotting your career plan. You must plan to achieve two major goals: to gain education and to gain experience.

In gearing your formal education to a career in information management, select a program in which information is a major component of the discipline. For example, the disciplines of information science, library science, computer science, business administration, public administration, journalism, communications, economics, and statistics place strong emphasis on the importance of information in business, industry, and government.

Although at this time there is no degree in information management, several graduate school programs have shown a strong concern for the subject. The following list is illustrative, not definitive.

University of California, Berkeley
  Graduate School of Business Administration
  School of Library and Information Studies

University of California, Los Angeles
  Graduate School of Library and Information Science
  Graduate School of Management

Carnegie Mellon University
  School of Library Science

University of Chicago
  Graduate Library School

Drexel University
  School of Library and Information Science

Georgia Institute of Technology
  School of Information and Computer Science

Harvard University
  Master of Information Science Program

University of Maryland
  College of Library and Information Services

Massachusetts Institute of Technology
Sloan School of Management

Michigan State University
Department of Communication

University of Minnesota
School of Business Administration

New York University
Graduate School of Business Administration

Ohio State University
Department of Computer and Information Science

University of Pennsylvania
Wharton School of Business

University of Pittsburgh
Graduate School of Library and Information Sciences

University of Southern California
Annenberg School of Communications

Stanford University
Graduate School of Business
Institute for Communication Research

Syracuse University
School of Information Studies

University of Texas
Graduate School of Business
Graduate School of Library Science

University of Washington
School of Communications

In addition to formal education, on-the-job training can prepare you for assuming the responsibilities of an information manager. Try to work for a company that has an information department and to get hands-on learning experience about the various facets of information management. When an opportunity opens for a top slot, you will be ready to compete for it. If the potential for growth seems limited, you can always use the fundamental knowledge you have acquired to accept a position with another firm.

You can acquire valuable experience in related jobs, and enter the field of information management via the back door. Specifically, there are four back doors that can lead to a career in information management for you. One includes jobs with the titles of librarian, archivist, and records manager—positions in which organization of information plays a major role. Another includes jobs called statistician, operations researcher, financial analyst, and marketing analyst—positions in which skills in interpreting and correlating data are integral components. A third job-title group clusters around information technology. Computer scientist, telecommunications manager, word processing manager, data processing manager, and reprographic manager are likely candidates for the broader area of information management. The communication skills embodied in job titles such as technical writer, technical editor, and journalist have also opened doors to careers in information management.

Many professional organizations and groups can be extremely helpful, not only in guiding you with career planning kits, but also in providing you with lists of current opportunities and announcing your availability to their members. The following list is indicative of some of the major information-oriented societies.

Associated Information Managers (A program of the
    Information Industry Association)
    316 Pennsylvania Avenue, S.E.
    Suite 502
    Washington, D.C. 20003

Special Libraries Association
    235 Park Avenue South
    New York, N.Y. 10003

American Society for Information Science
    1010 Sixteenth Street, N.W.
    Washington, D.C. 20036

Association of Records Managers and Administrators
    P.O. Box 281
    Bradford, R.I. 02808

Association for Computing Machinery
1133 Avenue of the Americas
New York, N.Y. 10036

Society for Technical Communication
1010 Vermont Avenue, N.W.
Suite 421
Washington, D.C. 20005

CAREER DEVELOPMENT

Marketing yourself and your services over a scheduled period of time is the essence of career development. There are three basic roadblocks that you will have to overcome during your career development: traditional, personal, and organizational.

Traditional roadblocks are the stereotypes that have evolved over the years regarding various professions. For example, the mousy librarian with pulled-back hair and eyeglasses is an updated version of another stereotyped librarian: the buxom woman, hair wadded into a bun, with right index finger pressed to her lips to enforce silence. Attendance at a convention of librarians or records managers quickly dispels such mythical characterizations and reveals an entirely different personification of librarians. Both men and women in information careers are tuned into on-line information retrieval systems, microforms, videotapes, and so on. Nevertheless, the stereotypes persist.

In one company the head librarian broached the idea of an on-line system to her boss. His first reaction was that she replace one of the professional library specialists with a library assistant, because he envisioned the terminal as being nothing more than a "fancy" typewriter keyboard—and of course all you need at a typewriter is a clerk-typist! She had to explain to him that she was requesting a professional information specialist who could set up complex search strategies, understand the indexing of more than 100 data bases, know how to expand a search or narrow an inquiry, and have the smarts to switch to different data bases for the information.

Operations researchers and statisticians have been pigeonholed into the image of number crunchers or bean counters, devoid of any human feelings or concerns. Computer scientists and telecommunications experts carry the burden of specialists or technicians who are only machine-oriented, and have no conception of managing the information needed by the company. The people who make up the communications groups are dubbed creative, arty, flighty; they're the loners who come up with the magic words and graphs for management but who are not management material. Stereotypes die hard. In order to overcome this career roadblock, you will have to change the way you are perceived by company executives.

Personal roadblocks are those you make yourself. To quote Pogo, "We have met the enemy and he is us." Just as organizations change to fit the times and to accommodate shifts in market preferences, so must you change to keep up with the times and with new demands for information. Have you allowed yourself to become professionally obsolete? Find out. If you earned your master's degree seven or more years ago and have since done nothing to update your knowledge, you have.

The need to establish credentials doesn't end when you don a cap and gown and accept your diploma. You must recertify yourself continually if you expect to compete successfully in the information industry.

But watch for potential hazards in keeping yourself up to date and getting the degrees to prove it. One person took a year's leave of absence from his company to earn a doctorate in information science. In December he defended his dissertation. In January he defended his job. His boss thought he was overqualified for handling the corporation's information center. He was told, in a positive way, that someone with a doctorate should be using it to do something more than running the information center. The information center manager quickly responded that he would apply his new knowledge to expand the information center's functions and to assume greater responsibilities for the company's information needs than before. He was not about to change positions or jobs; rather he planned to change the job to make it more responsive to the company's needs and wants. By presenting his case convincingly, he was able to change his boss's mind and keep his job. Just as traditional stereotypes may be hazardous to your career, so, too, may your formal credentials.

As regards organizational roadblocks, don't be bound in by the organizational hierarchy in which you are thrust. Promote and market your services throughout the corporation. This is important for you and for those you serve. Let them know you are there to help them solve problems. Make them aware that you are an anticipator of information needs rather than a responder to requests. Establish a reputation for being a clearinghouse so that you can refer people to others in the organization who can help them. Build up a strong collection of information so that it is speedily available when it's needed. Let others know yours is a mobile service with portable terminals—ready and able to go to them when the information demands require it.

Career Tracks and Salaries

A typical career track for an information manager has five stations. The entry level is that of a trainee. The next stop is a staff member. With education, training, and experience you move up to senior member. Demonstrating your ability to head up a group takes you to the supervisory level. The ultimate destination is that of an information manager.

Pay scales in 1981 for a trainee range from $9,280 to $16,704. Staff members top out at $24,128, and the senior level upper limit is $31,552. Supervisors may earn as high as $38,976. The information manager with broad services has an upper limit of $46,400. Obviously these five levels overlap in pay scales and salaries will vary depending on geographic location, industry, company, and job responsibilities. (These figures are based on a survey conducted by the Information Industry Association in 1977; they have been adjusted for merit increases and inflation.)

Of course, a person with equivalent experience and training that dovetails with the information department's professional needs need not enter at the trainee level. Mid-career changes will easily bring a person onto the career track at the staff member or senior member level and occasionally into a supervisory position. Plan to spend two to three years in early jobs and five years or so in later assignments.

CONTINGENCY PLANS

As Scotland's laureate poet Robbie Burns so wisely wrote, "The best laid schemes o' mice and men gang aft a-gley." The wise planner will develop contingency plans to follow if initial plans are thwarted and blocked. Although perseverance, diligence, and assertiveness are qualities that will speed up your career, some employees on the fast track will try to reach their ultimate destination at the expense of the company. They get derailed in most instances. Their personal goals diverge from company goals and they soon find themselves stopped in their own tracks by their own opportunistic devices.

You may also find that your company is not information oriented and its policies and procedures will not change. One warning of danger is the false- or inflated-title syndrome, in which you have the title of information manager or director, but are treated as record keeper, with little or no authority or responsibility. Another warning signal is if, after a year or so, you realize that you are on a circular track; 20 years from now you will have had one year of experience repeated 20 times.

Such situations demand that you set up alternative routes for your trip to the top. Transfer into another department, change employers, join another industry—even go into business for yourself as an information broker or consultant. The contingency plan is something that only you can develop. But it is critical to your success. (Without it you may find yourself in a highly vulnerable position.)

The position of information manager can be very rewarding. But it does require you to sit down and set up your own program. You can be among the first to shape and form your own career in a burgeoning and stimulating profession. The Age of Information offers you the opportunity to pioneer in a fast-moving, upwardly mobile profession. Only you can make the choice.

REFERENCES

1. Henry C. Lucas, Jr., "Preparing Executives for Corporate Information Management," *Infosystems,* October 1979, p. 114.
2. © 1979 Dr. Morton F. Meltzer.

10

INFORMATION MANAGEMENT—THE LARGER PERSPECTIVE

The corporations that will excel in the 1980s will be those that manage information as a major resource.[1]

—*John Diebold*

The information manager has an all-encompassing responsibility for the information needs of his organization. In his capacity as information manager he must be objective. He must broadly view information as a resource, critically look at the organization's total information needs from within, and sharply focus on his company's information needs from an outside position. To obtain these three perspectives, the information manager must assume several roles.

ORGANIZATIONAL ENTREPRENEUR

Your role as an organizational entrepreneur requires that you organize, manage, and assume the risks and rewards of your company. You do not work for your organization, you work with it. You are a partner of the corporation. You are a decision maker and problem solver in all aspects of the company's operations and participate in the planning and setting of corporate goals.

Effective and efficient information flow within your company is your responsibility. You must exercise your authority to open up all the channels of communication within your organization. This requires your involvement in every department. Other division managers may complain that you are invading their turf. Resolve this conflict quickly by showing how your operation will help them do a better job and make the company more successful. Information is interdivisional in nature and must not be blocked by an arbitrary organizational structure.

Consider personal privacy as an example. Assuredly, company policies about employee records should remain the responsibility of the personnel or human resources department. But it is up to the information manager to alert top-level management (including the personnel director) about any forces, events, and trends that will make information about personnel a major issue of the 1980s. Facing up to potential problems before they become reality will prevent a "management by crisis" syndrome and further government intrusion into your business. As the information manager you must alert your company to these signs on the horizon.

In May 1979, Louis Harris & Associates, Inc., published *A National Opinion Research Survey of Attitudes Toward Privacy.* The survey, based on 2,131 interviews representing a cross-section of American adults, included 618 representatives of leadership groups such as congressmen, business executives, and regulatory officials. More than 80 percent of the respondents agreed that "Americans begin surrendering their personal privacy the day they open up their first charge account, take out a loan, buy something on the installment plan, or apply for a credit card."

As regards employee–employer relationships, 92 percent of the public felt that employers should have a specific policy designed to protect the information in employee personnel and medical files. Eighty-three percent of the public felt it is very important that the employer inform the employee before revealing any personal information from the employee's files (with the exception of regular reporting required by law.) Seventy percent of the public thought a law should be passed to specify employee rights of access to their personnel files and that the employer should not determine those rights.

Unless business and private industry initiate policies to protect the privacy of their customers and employees, legislation may force companies to comply with costly, strict regulations. California, Maine, Michigan, Oregon, and Pennsylvania already have laws giving employees in the private sector the right to inspect their personnel records. And on April 2, 1979, President Carter sent a policy statement to Congress to protect individual privacy. He stated, "It is time to establish a broad, national privacy policy to protect individual rights in the Information Age." He proposed that the privacy policy be based on two principles:

> *Fair Information Practices.* Standards must be provided for handling sensitive, personal records. Individuals should be told what kind of information is being collected about them, how it will be used, and to whom it will be disclosed. They should be able to see and obtain a copy of the records and correct any errors. They should be told the basis for an adverse decision that may be based on personal data. And they should be able to prevent improper access to the records.
>
> *Limits on the Government.* Government access to and use of personal information must be limited and supervised so that power over information cannot be used to threaten our liberties.

You, the information manager, must address this issue of privacy in your role of organizational entrepreneur. Think like a chief executive officer. Face the broad issues that involve your organization. View the privacy issue as an information problem—not just a personnel problem. It is this larger perspective of information that establishes you, the information manager, in a vital role in the modern organization. Many internal and external issues that face your company should be reevaluated in this light. Other groups may implement the policies that emerge from these changes, but you must take the initiative in presenting these problems and providing solutions to other top executives in your organization.

PROVIDER AND USER OF INFORMATION

In your role of information provider and user you must think of various ways you will process the economic resource information, consider the internal needs for information to make the organization run more effectively, and be aware of the external demands for information from the various publics the organization deals with. Old-line thinking would restrict the processing of information to three major categories: acquisition, maintenance, and distribution. With the arrival of the Age of Information, business and government now realize there are other aspects to consider. These include synthesis, analysis, and evaluation of the information, which in turn produce new information. By monitoring competitors' activities, changes in customers' preferences, and legislative actions, new information is brought to light. There are needs to protect information and remove outdated material. You must involve yourself with all these activities in your role as a provider and user of information.

The Freedom of Information Act (1966) is a good example of an outside force impacting the internal operations of a company and affecting the processing of information. The Act states that "any person"—defined to include corporations and other business entities as well as individuals—should have access to identifiable government records without having to show a need or even a reason. The "need-to-know standard" is replaced with the "right-to-know doctrine." The burden of proof for withholding information is placed on the government. The 1974 amendments to the Act speed up the response time and ease the process of requesting information.

The Freedom of Information Act applies only to documents held by the administrative agencies of the executive branch of the federal government. This means you have the right to see information held by military departments, government corporations, and independent regulatory agencies, as well as executive departments and officers.

You will find the federal government is a rich source of information. When the information you seek has not been published and is not available through other channels, you can request the information under the Freedom of Information Act. For example, the Agriculture Department has data on the purity and quality of meat and poultry products and the harmful effects of pesticides. Records of regulatory agencies deal with air pollution control, safety records of airlines, and the adverse effects of television violence. There are test results on the nutritional content of processed foods, the efficacy of drugs, and the safety and efficiency of all makes of automobiles. Consumer complaints registered with the Federal Trade Commission about interstate moving companies, corporate marketing policies, and faulty products are also available.

There are those in business and industry who may feel that requesting such information under the Freedom of Information Act should fall under the jurisdiction of the legal department. Not so! The responsibility for acquiring information and providing it to your users is yours as information manager. This does not mean you should not consult with the legal department for advice and guidance; it does mean the authority is yours to use. When information is denied and you wish to file an appeal, the legal department can be of great assistance to you. It can provide you with citations of court rulings as to why the agency's use of a particular exemption to withhold information is inappropriate. If the agency denies your appeal and your company is willing to take the case to court, then the matter should be handled by legal counsel. At this juncture it is no longer a matter of obtaining information, but becomes a case requiring the skills of professional lawyers with expertise in federal practice.

Government agencies can refuse to disclose information if it falls within one of nine categories:

1. *Classified documents concerning national defense and foreign policy.* The mere fact that information is classified does not automatically exempt it from disclosure. The burden is on the government to convince the court that the document in question is correctly classified.

2. *Internal personnel rules and practices of a government agency.* If such documents affect interests outside the agency or deal with procedures that are not confined to internal rules and practices, they must be released in spite of this exemption.

3. *Information exempt under other laws.* Examples of such types of information include income tax returns, patent applications, and records about nuclear testing.

4. *Confidential business information.* This exemption protects from disclosure "trade secrets and commercial or financial information obtained from a person and privileged confidential." The consensus of judicial opinion is that it does not apply to general information obtained by the government with the understanding that it will be held in confidence.

Trade secrets pertain to such things as processes, formulas, manufacturing plans, and chemical compositions. Commercial and financial information includes corporate sales data, salaries and bonuses of industry personnel, and bids received by corporations in the course of their acquisitions. However, commercial and financial information other than trade secrets can be withheld from disclosure only if such information meets certain criteria: it must be privileged and confidential and it must be obtained from a "person" by the government.

The courts have defined "confidential" information as that information which if disclosed would be likely to impair the government's ability to obtain similar information in the future or harm the competitive position of the person who supplied it. Information obtained from a "person" includes data supplied by corporations and partnerships as well as individual citizens. It does not apply to records generated by the government, such as government-prepared documents based on government information.

There have been a number of instances in which corporations that have submitted information to government departments and agencies have later appealed to the courts to issue injunctions against disclosure of the information to others. These are referred to as "reverse" Freedom of Information cases.

Two Chrysler Corporation workers invoked the Freedom of Information Act to obtain affirmative action plans that Chrysler had filed with the Defense Logistics Agency. Chrysler filed a "reverse" Freedom of Information Act suit to prevent disclosure of the information, citing exemption #4—that private, confidential information need not be turned over to the requestor. Chrysler contended that its affirmative action plans would reveal to competitors its expansion strategies, that the plan revealed where it expected to increase its labor force.

On April 18, 1979, the U.S. Supreme Court in *Chrysler vs. Brown* ruled against Chrysler. In essence it was judged that the Freedom of

Information Act is only a disclosure statute. The exemptions are for the discretionary use of the government agencies, not for providers of information to use to prevent disclosure.

5. *Internal communications.* This exemption safeguards the policy-making processes of government. It states that interagency or intra-agency memos and letters that reflect predecisional attitudes about policy alternatives need not be disclosed. However, communications about decisions already made must be released.

6. *Protection of privacy.* This covers personnel and medical files and records that would clearly be an unwarranted invasion of a person's privacy if disclosed.

7. *Investigatory files.* Records compiled for law enforcement purposes must be released unless their disclosure would result in one or more of six specific harms: deprive a person of the right to a fair trial, endanger the life of law enforcement personnel, interfere with enforcement proceedings, constitute an unwarranted invasion of personal privacy, disclose the identity of a confidential source, or disclose investigative techniques and procedures.

8. *Information concerning financial institutions.* Federal agencies responsible for the regulation or supervision of financial institutions do not have to release material contained in the examination, operating, or condition reports they prepare. For example, an investigatory report of the Federal Reserve Board about federal banks would be exempt.

9. *Information about wells.* This last exemption states that geologic and geophysical information and data (including maps) concerning wells are exempt from the Freedom of Information Act. This is a further refinement of the trade-secret provision of this Act.

As a provider and user of information, you will view the Freedom of Information Act as a double-edged sword. It is an excellent tool to uncover information about other companies and government agencies, but it can also be invoked by others to find out information about your company's operations. You must alert your company to the consequences of providing certain types of information to government agencies. Be aware of any requests to government agencies for information about your company, and prepare policies to deal with the Freedom of Information Act and all its consequences. Marketing people may need the information, company lawyers may become involved, accountants and employees in personnel departments may want to prevent government disclosure of information—but it is the information manager who must be the linchpin in dealing with the myriad aspects of this and other information problems.

POLICY MAKER

As information manager you will set policy regarding the information resources of your organization. Policy making is an inherent responsibility of the job. If you are not in a position to authorize a policy statement, you must advise and persuade those who are in such a position to act on your suggestions. Some information managers feel that policy formulation is beyond their organizational level. Their low position on the organization chart may make them feel they can make no major contribution to policy formulation. Such an attitude is self-defeating.

The interrelationships between information and such internal and external interests as telecommunications, data processing, word processing, personal privacy issues, corporate confidentiality, new products and services, and designation of new markets compel the formulation of information policies. How your company handles information determines the quality of the decisions your corporation makes.

The creation of information within your organization is one area that demands a policy statement. Without such policy a chaotic, undirected approach to innovation emerges. You must orient your employees to the long-term goals of the corporation so that they can channel their creative talents to fulfill these objectives. The engineering division, and particularly the research and development departments, will both make major contributions to such a policy, but the information manager must contribute his significant statements also. Information is the basis for the creation of new information. And it is imperative that you be a part of this policy-making decision.

The acquisition of information is an area of policy formulation in which the information manager plays a prime role. The collation of the information collection is the responsibility of the information manager. It is essential that an information policy statement clearly declares that the information manager is responsible for coordinating the information resources of the organization. The critical word is coordinating. The intent is not to create an information czar within the organization, but rather to bring together all the information resources of a company so that it may accomplish its missions and reach its goals.

Information dissemination cries out for a policy initiative. Effective and efficient information flow in a corporation is essential to success. Many companies have a vast quantity of procedures by which they communicate various kinds of information throughout their organizations. Few have issued policy statements mandating that information will be disseminated to ensure a well-informed management.

Availability of and access to information are two more policy areas that top management must address. The availability issue requires that the information manager be kept informed as to what kinds of information are already in-house and what kinds of new information are being generated on various programs and projects. The information manager must have the responsibility and authority to maintain a perpetual inventory of available information within the organization, wherever it may be located. In essence, the information manager is an information gatekeeper. There must be a corollary policy that ensures access to the available information. No company can condone the information hoarder. And certainly no company can afford to support one. Access to information must be spelled out as a management right with a parallel responsibility to safeguard it against unethical use.

In policy statements, encourage the use of information. Unless you stimulate employees to put information to work, productivity will lag and profits will diminish. Top management must declare a company policy that encompasses the concept of information utilization.

Walter A. Kleinschrod, editor of *Administrative Management,* addressed the subject of information policy in a November 1978 editorial in his publication.

> Who in the organization will evaluate and interpret information before the users get it? That person holds power in his hands. What shall be our policies on disclosure and privacy, and who will be responsible for keeping information secure? Who will determine what may be released? These people face legal and technological challenges far greater than any encountered before. Who *owns* information? That question tests not only the strength of the copyright law and government agencies which enforce it, but also the viability of emerging "information industries" which supply business with all manner of products and services.
>
> Questions like these plainly go beyond simple storage or retrieval and the other routines of information handling. They reach to a web of larger issues surrounding the whole life-cycle of information in its creation, use, and eventual discard. They touch the intrinsic nature of information itself. This larger context compels organizations to recognize a need for comprehensive information policies, the kinds of policies our would-be information managers must forge.[2]

Obviously, information policy issues cross over the entire operations of an organization. It is this larger perspective of information management that is necessary for a viable organization to be successful. Therefore your role in formulating information policy is critical.

AGENT OF CHANGE

In your role as an agent of change, you must have access to the capital and labor resources of your company to accomplish corporate objectives. Efficient use of personnel and equipment must be coordinated with information resources.

You need to set forth an information capability plan to delineate what the state of the art is as regards information management. You must compare the current status of your organization with the state of the art. Next, decide where you want to be in five or ten years from now. Finally, draw up plans for achieving that position. As an individual who is linked with one of the most dynamic growth industries in the United States, you must take the initiative in incorporating those elements of information technology and resources that will ensure that your company is competitive now and in the future. This means you must experiment with new concepts and tools in information science. Adopt those that are feasible and adapt others to meet the information needs of your organization.

Much new information science work is going on in academia, government laboratories, and the private sector of the information industry. Keep abreast of these developments and inform your key executives of any breakthroughs that will affect your company's operations in dealing with consumers, other companies, and the government. Let your chief executive officer know how much money information will cost, but show that it is also profitable. Preparing the groundwork for accepting changes is a necessary part of your job as the information manager.

As an agent of change you must realize that your own area of responsibility will change over time. For example, nonbibliographic data bases are becoming more prevalent and are frequently marketed to the end user. The information in these data bases usually can be manipulated so that the format of the final report best meets the end user's needs. Nearly 80 percent of these bases are searched directly by end users.

This does not herald the end of the information center. It does mean the information manager must make sure that through information policies and procedures he will be responsible for acquiring such data bases. This will avoid duplication, prevent a proliferation of incompatible computer terminals, and ensure control of the equipment and data bases within your organization.

You must keep current with new information products as they become available. You must alert potential end users of these services, acquire access to data bases that your organization needs, and maintain a "key-person file" listing the people who are using them. Even though these services may be purchased with the departmental funds of the end users, the ultimate source of these funds is the organization itself. Anyone in the organization with a need to know should have access to these information resources.

OTHER ROLES

The role of organization coordinator pervades the other roles of the information manager. To this is added the role of researcher, which you assume when you experiment with new information technology. The role of resource mobilizer becomes part of your repertoire as you gain official authority and influence in your company to commit capital, equipment, and manpower to perform the ever-broadening responsibilities you will assume.

As a mover and shaker who views information management from this larger perspective, you will prove to be a profit maker for your organization.

REFERENCES

1. John Diebold, Chairman, The Diebold Group, Inc. "IRM: New Directions in Management," *Infosystems,* October 1979, p. 41.
2. Walter A. Kleinschrod, "All That Information But Very Few Policies for Managing It," *Administrative Management,* November 1978, p. 25. Copyright © 1978 by Geyer-McAllister Publications, Inc., New York.

11

MANAGEMENT DOCTRINES AND PRINCIPLES

The ability to convert business information to sound judg-
ments is distinctively human. Even that intuitive, gut-level,
"sixth sense" that we sometimes call "a good head for
business" is actually the ability to assimilate and analyze
information so quickly as to seem unconscious.[1]
—William I. Spencer

Most management books begin with theories, philosophies, and concepts. I have deliberately chosen to end this book with management doctrines and principles based on experience and research applicable to the emerging Age of Information. The reason: like the Age of Information, these principles are just developing. In essence, this book does not come to a close, but opens up a whole new era. Managers can use these guidelines in coping with problems, making decisions, and planning the future in a new work environment.

REVIEW OF MANAGEMENT THOUGHT

A body of management knowledge has developed over the past 80 years in the Industrial Society. This evolution of management thought covers the ideas of Frederick W. Taylor, father of scientific management early in this century, through the 1927 classic studies at the Hawthorne Plant at Western Electric Company in which the importance of human relations in organizations was first highlighted. This was followed after World War II with management concepts dealing with quantification and systems theory.

There have been several attempts to classify management functions. In 1916 Henri Fayol, the French industrialist, introduced five factors of management in the title of his book, *Administration Industrielle et Generale—Prevoyance, Organisation, Commandement, Coordination, Controle;* that is, planning, organizing, commanding, coordinating, and controlling. In 1937 Luther Gulick expanded Fayol's theory in a paper, "The Theory of Organization," as part of the Brownlow Committee's volume, *Papers on the Science of Administration.* The famous acronym POSDCORB summed up Gulick's seven responsibilities of administrative management: planning, organizing, staffing, directing, coordinating, reporting, and budgeting. And in another classic, written in 1938, *The Functions of the Executive,* Chester I. Barnard listed three essential activities: provide a system of communication, secure essential efforts or services from individuals, and formulate and define purpose.

Catchy titles describing management fashions, politics, and trends have appeared on the scene in the last three decades. Stephen Potter published his *Theory and Practice of Gamesmanship* in 1947, *Some Notes on Lifesmanship* in 1950, and *One-upmanship* in 1952. C. Northcote Parkinson formulated a law: work expands to fill the time available, and made it the title of a book, *Parkinson's Law.* In 1969, Laurence J. Peter introduced the Peter Principle, which states that, "in a hierarchy, every employee tends to rise to his level of incompetence." Even more pithy "laws" and "principles" continue to titillate the public's desire for aphorisms and simple solutions.

DOCTRINES OF INFORMATION MANAGEMENT

In a more serious tone, former Senator George McGovern straightforwardly defines the difference between policy and doctrine.

> There is an important difference between a policy and a doctrine. A policy is good for as long as it works or is needed, whereupon, without undue difficulty, it can be altered or discarded. When a policy is finished, it is not the end of an era; it is merely the end of an approach that has outlived its usefulness. A doctrine, by contrast, is for the ages, and is neither easily nor safely trifled with, even when it has outlived its usefulness or acquired unintended meanings.[2]

This explains why there are few doctrines that relate directly to the management of organizations, and even fewer that deal directly with information and its role in management.

Information is the ultimate management resource. Francis Bacon paraphrased this doctrine as "knowledge is power" in 1597; nearly 400 years later it remains a basic tenet for those who must manage. The word "power" might seem too authoritarian a term in this age of participative management and theoretically more democratically run organizations. Yet a manager must have the power or authority to make decisions, direct operations, and formulate plans. Such actions must be based on the best information available. If, through a series of failures or inactions, it becomes apparent that an individual manages by vested power only and not by informed thought processes, he will soon lose his power. Superiors will remove him from his managerial position, peers will soon dissociate themselves from him, and subordinates will ignore his mandates. A manager maintains authority by demonstrating his ability to put information to work. Information *is* the ultimate management resource and it pervades every activity of management. As Arnold E. Keller, editorial director of *Infosystems,* has declared, "Without question, information is the essence of effective management."[3]

Information is a personal, organizational, and national resource. This book has devoted an entire chapter to this doctrine. Information has great value. It is bought and sold in the marketplaces of the world. Unlike other resources, it is not depleted as it is used. The more information is used, the more valuable it becomes. American business thrives on information in our competitive environment. As David T. Kearns, president and chief operating officer of Xerox Corporation, has written, "The one great lie in this country—and it has to be exposed—is that it's all over for us. . . . I don't agree, not just because I find it totally unacceptable, but because I believe it's totally avoidable. The wealth, at least of this nation, is not in the ground. It's in our minds—and that is a renewable resource. We can create new wealth, and we have."[4]

Information is a basic human need. Even the most primitive tribes need information to survive—information on what food is safe to gather and eat, how to obtain it, and (as they become more civilized), how to grow it. In the business organization there is a hunger for information that must be satisfied if the organization is to survive. Different levels of management require different types of information to function; and nonmanagement personnel need information to operate effectively in the organizational framework. It is management's responsibility to ensure that the company's information needs are satisfied.

PRINCIPLES OF INFORMATION MANAGEMENT

Henri Fayol listed 14 principles of management in his book. Most of these are still valid. For example, he proposed that authority and responsibility be made complementary managerial duties. His statement on remuneration—that employees should be rewarded fairly and reasonably for their efforts—is still applicable. But other principles he promoted have not fared as well. His concept of unity of command, which declares that an employee should have but one supervisor, has been challenged. New approaches such as the matrix organization (where an information specialist may report to both a project manager as well as an information manager) is a case in point. His statement on subordination of individual interest to general interest must be modified to adapt to a society in which an employee's values and an organization's goals are integrated to achieve mutually profitable objectives.

Just as Fayol's principles of management were valuable, principles of information management are needed as guidelines to help managers do their jobs effectively and efficiently in today's information-oriented world. Avoid the idea that any such principles are cast in concrete; to be effective, they must be flexible and adaptable to the needs of managers. They are not offered as an exhaustive, all-encompassing dictum of management conduct, but are a suggested list of sound management practices. They provide a solid basis for management actions where the management of information and knowledge workers is as critical as the management of financial and physical resources.

1. *Utilization of Information.* Information must be put to work. The acquisition, processing, and distribution of information are

wasted efforts if the information is not used to its best advantage. The effective manager must initiate suggestions and stimulate ideas about how to use the information. He or she must create an information-supportive climate to allow knowledge workers to use the information in innovative ways.

2. *Access to Information.* You must encourage access to information in your organization. Minimize the efforts of your knowledge workers to obtain information. If the effort to obtain the information is greater than the need for it, the information will either be obtained through another (easier) avenue or not be obtained at all.

3. *Safeguards.* You must set up safeguards to protect the rights of individuals and the organization as they relate to the acquisition of information. This does not negate the principle of information access, but reinforces the doctrine of information as a resource. You must distinguish between requests that are based on a need to know and those based on a "want to know." Want-to-know information should still be provided, but always within the context of privacy considerations.

4. *Centralization and Decentralization of Information.* Centralization of information policy making and processing is an efficient, effective, and economic practice in this fast-changing world of information proliferation. Decentralization of information systems, whether they're manual, automated, or computerized, brings the information source closer to the ultimate user and must be encouraged.

5. *Anticipating Information.* The information manager must anticipate information needs and not just react to information requests. This form of contingency planning in information is vital where time is of the essence in responding to requests for proposals and formulating marketing plans. Anticipating information goes beyond acquiring the information itself. It extends to awareness of information sources that can be quickly tapped when the information is needed.

6. *Information Format.* Information must be presented in the format that best meets the needs of the user, not the format that is most convenient for the information department or best meets the demands of information technology. Top-level managers need the

broad coverage that results from analysis, synthesis, and evaluation. Middle-level supervisors need more detailed information that includes the goals set by top management. First-line supervisors need information to help them fulfill their operating responsibilities within the framework of the organization's aims. Dumping of reams of computer printouts on managers' desks burdens the users with irrelevant information that hampers their jobs.

7. *Information and the Manager's Span of Control.* Information technology now permits managers to control a wider range of activities and to effectively supervise twice as many subordinates as they could before. This increase in span of control helps to make organizations more horizontal in structure and thus improves communications within the organization.

8. *Accepting Information.* Managers must develop an open-minded attitude toward new information, even when the information may contradict their prior decisions, opinions, and beliefs. To get the facts is one thing. But the managers must face those facts and use them in planning, organizing, directing, coordinating, and controlling operations. Information that was once valid may be augmented, changed, or even proved invalid with the development of new situations and changing events.

9. *Information Flow.* Information, like air, must flow upward, downward, and across all levels of management, and must even extend outside the organization. The pyramidal organizational structure in which information slowly filters downward through a series of management sieves is not feasible in today's modern organization—if it ever was. Today all members must be aware of what is going on and how they should contribute to the overall goals of the company. Management must listen to the information provided by nonmanagement personnel, customers, and other groups outside the formal organization.

10. *Recognition of the Information Manager.* Recognition of the need for an information manager to manage the information resources of an organization is paramount, or everyone's responsibility will become no one's responsibility. The information manager must report directly to the highest level of the corporation so that he can determine firsthand what the corporation's information needs

are and can also provide unfiltered information directly to top-level management. The information manager must be recognized as an integral part of the organization and must receive more than just a job title and an office. The highest levels of the corporation must support the information manager publicly and financially.

11. *Information as an Agent of Change.* Current and future actions are usually constrained by past decisions. New information can provide a larger repertoire of choices for managers as well as support for changes that negate or severely alter past decisions. Plans and programs must be based on how things are, not on how they were when the projected plans were initiated. Information on new regulations, declining or emerging markets, and technical breakthroughs must be collected, analyzed, and distributed by the information manager. Information is a force for change as well as a reinforcer of good decisions.

12. *Information and Productivity.* Productivity improvement is based on working smarter—not harder. This calls for well-informed managers who can incorporate new ideas to increase output by lowering labor and capital expenses.

13. *Information as a Motivator.* When employees are kept informed as to what is expected of them, how the company is doing, and what the general aims and purposes of the corporation are, they are motivated to meet or exceed expectations. People want to achieve and excel. But to attain their goals, they must know what the goals are. Also, being informed gives an employee a sense of participation, which in turn motivates him to succeed.

14. *Information Requires Investments.* Managers must commit capital and labor to maintain an up-to-date level of information. Professional people, information, and information technology must comprise the information center. These all cost money. But members of the organization will be more apt to use information facilities if they have confidence in the information manager and the center's professional staff.

15. *Information Requires Management Insight.* No matter how quantitative or clinical the information is, managers must still use their education, training, experience, and management insight to put information to work most effectively. The manager's job is one

that requires information, but information needs managers who have the vision and foresight to use this most valuable resource. The doctrines and principles enumerated here are not only for information managers but must be applied by all managers and administrators in business, industry, and government. These concepts augment and amplify good management practices that have proved profitable in the Industrial Age. Other thoughts are distilled from ideas that were presented throughout this book, which is set in the context of the Age of Information. We are not operating in a time of crisis, turbulence, or revolution. The shift from an industrial-based economy to an information-oriented society is an orderly transition. As a manager you will find this new era even more challenging and rewarding. You will be integrating the contributions of knowledge workers, information, and information technology to fulfill the needs of the Age of Information. The opportunities are limitless, for you have at your disposal the ultimate management resource: information.

REFERENCES

1. William I. Spencer, "What Do Upper Executives Want from MIS?" *Administrative Management,* July 1978, p. 68. Copyright © 1978 by Geyer-McAllister Publications Inc., New York.
2. George McGovern, "How to Avert a New 'Cold War,'" *The Atlantic Monthly,* June 1980, p. 45. Copyright 1980, by The Atlantic Monthly Company, Boston, Mass. Reprinted by Permission.
3. Arnold E. Keller, "The Need to Know," *Infosystems,* June 1979, p. 3.
4. David T. Kearns, "Let's Take Risks Again," *Newsweek,* May 5, 1980, p. 13. Copyright 1980, by Newsweek, Inc. All Rights Reserved. Reprinted by Permission.

Part IV:
Information Source Book

A

SELECTED LIST OF DATA BASES

This list of data bases is by no means comprehensive. The information is provided to alert you to the different types of information available through various data base vendors. Complete listings, current costs, and more detailed descriptions can be obtained from a number of sources. The following three vendors are especially valuable information sources, and I will refer to them throughout this section in abbreviated form.

> **Bibliographic Retrieval Services, Inc. (BRS)**
> 702 Corporation Park
> Scotia, NY 12302
> (518) 374-5011

> **Lockheed Information Systems (LIS)**
> DIALOG
> 3460 Hillview Avenue
> Palo Alto, CA 94304
> (415) 493-4411

System Development Corporation (SDC)
SDC Search Service—ORBIT
2500 Colorado Avenue
Santa Monica, CA 90406
(800) 421-7229

Directories listing more than 700 commercial information services, data bases, and data services are available through Telenet and Tymnet data communication networks.

Telenet Communications Corporation
8229 Boone Boulevard
Vienna, VA 22180
(703) 827-9565

Tymnet, Inc.
20665 Valley Green Drive
Cupertino, CA 95014
(408) 446-7000

BUSINESS OPPORTUNITIES

ABI/Inform Abstracted business information (ABI) covers all areas of business management and administration as given in 400 publications.

Time Span: 1971–present. Updated monthly.
Number of records: 107,000.
Available through: BRS; LIS; SDC.

Accountants Index Information on the complete spectrum of accounting (such as auditing, taxation, data processing, and management) both in the United States and overseas is contained in this data base prepared by the American Institute of Certified Public Accountants.

Time span: 1974–present. Updated quarterly.
Number of records: 12,000.
Available through: SDC.

Chemical Industry Notes Extracts of articles from 75 domestic and foreign periodicals covering the chemical processing industry. Oriented to business topics such as corporate activities, prices, and sales.

Time span: 1974–present. Updated biweekly.
Number of records: 294,000.
Available through: LIS; SDC.

Disclosure Extracts of all reports filed with the Securities and Exchange Commission are available through this data base. 10-K, 20-K, and 10-Q financial reports, 8-K reports of material events or unscheduled corporate changes, as well as proxy statements, registration reports, and so on are covered. More than 11,000 publicly owned companies can be searched. Microfiche copies of reports are available.

Time span: 1977–present. Updated weekly.
Number of records: 18,000.
Available through: LIS; Disclosure, Inc., 4827 Rugby
Avenue, Bethesda, MD 20014; (301) 951-0100.

Economics Abstracts International Produced in London, England, this data base covers such fields of economic science and management as markets, industries, and economic data of individual countries. Information is abstracted from 1,800 journals worldwide as well as reports, books, and directories.

Time span: 1974–present. Updated monthly.
Number of records: 89,000.
Available through: LIS.

EIS Industrial Plants More than 90 percent of U.S. industrial activity is covered in this data base. Information on 130,000 plants operated by 67,000 firms with annual sales greater than $500,000 is provided.

Time span: Current. Replaced every four months.
Number of records: 140,000.
Available through: LIS.

EIS Nonmanufacturing Establishments   Roughly 200,000 non-manufacturing establishments with 20 or more employees are listed. Such information as headquarter's name, location, percent of industry sales, industry classification, and so on are provided.

Time span: Current. Replaced every four months.
Number of records: 247,000.
Available through: LIS.

Federal Index   Information about federal legislation and regulations, contract awards, court decisions, and hearings are contained in this data base.

Time span: 1976–present. Updated monthly.
Number of records: 130,000.
Available through: BRS; LIS; SDC.

Foreign Traders Index   Compiled by the U.S. Department of Commerce, this data base lists firms in 130 countries outside of the United States which import United States goods or wish to represent U.S. exporters. The product or service of the firm; type of business activity such as wholesaling, manufacturing, etc.; key persons; size of the company; and date of establishment are provided.

Time span: Current five years. Updated quarterly.
Number of records: 155,000.
Available through: LIS.

Foundation Grants Index   This data base is helpful in determining the amounts and types of grants awarded by more than 400 U.S. foundations. Although most of the grants are awarded in the field of education, other areas such as science, health, and international activities receive many of the foundations' sponsorship. Grants of more than $5,000 to organizations (not individuals) are included.

Time span: 1973–present. Updated bimonthly.
Number of records: 68,000.
Available through: LIS.

Frost & Sullivan DM[2] Defense Market Measures System helps managers analyze and forecast the U.S. government as a market. It contains information on contract awards, sole-source negotiations, requests for proposals, planned procurement, and research and development needs.

> Time span: 1975–present. Updated quarterly.
> Number of records: 271,000.
> Available through: LIS.

Grants Database This data base produced by Oryx Press covers government, private sector, and not-for-profit organizations that offer grant programs. More than 1,500 grants are listed in over 88 disciplines.

> Time span: Current. Updated monthly.
> Number of records: 1,500.
> Available through: LIS; SDC.

Management Contents Abstracts of articles from 200 domestic and foreign journals, transactions, and proceedings dealing with all areas of management are accessible through this data base.

> Time span: 1974–present. Updated monthly.
> Number of records: 63,000.
> Available through: BRS; LIS; SDC.

Pharmaceutical News Index PNI provides on-line access to drug industry news found in eight publications and newsletters. In addition to news about drugs, cosmetics, and medical devices, it also contains references to articles on drug industry sales, corporate activities, court actions, and government regulations.

> Time span: 1975–present. Updated monthly.
> Number of records: 43,000.
> Available through: BRS; LIS.

Predicasts F&S Indexes Market planners and analysts will find information about domestic and interntional companies, industries, and products in this data base. Summaries of reports by security analysts, forecasts of sales and profits by corporate officials, and other significant business information are included.

> Time span: 1972–present. Updated monthly.
> Number of records: 1,470,000.
> Available through: BRS; LIS.

Predicasts International Forecasts This data base offers abstracts of published forecasts for all countries, except the United States. More than 1,000 sources are used to provide information on economics, industries, products, and end-use data.

> Time span: 1971–present. Updated monthly.
> Number of records: 323,000.
> Available through: LIS.

Predicasts International Time Series Demographic, economic, industrial, and product information is assembled in this data base, which covers 2,500 forecast time series on 50 major foreign countries. In addition, there are annual data for about 125,000 series for all countries of the world.

> Time span: 1972–present. Updated quarterly.
> Number of records: 118,000.
> Available through: BRS; LIS.

Predicasts PROMT Predicasts Overview of Markets and Technology contains worldwide information about products, technology, acquisitions, research and development, sales and earnings, market data, government regulations, and so forth.

> Time span: 1972–present. Updated monthly.
> Number of records: 305,000.
> Available through: BRS; LIS; SDC.

Predicasts U.S. Forecasts Abstracts of forecasts for the United States that have appeared in government publications, trade journals, and business periodicals make up this data base. Each entry usually contains historical data and short-term and long-term forecasts on industries, end-use distribution, and economics.

Time span: 1971–present. Updated quarterly.
Number of records: 196,000.
Available through: LIS.

Predicasts U.S. Time Series. This data base has two parts. The composites file contains 500 time series on the United States, with historical data from 1957 to projections through 1990. The basebook file is composed of 30,000 series on U.S. foreign trade, wages, production, consumption, prices, and so forth, dating from 1957.

Time span: 1971–present. Updated monthly.
Number of records: 35,000.
Available through: LIS.

Trade Opportunities This data base, produced by the U.S. Department of Commerce, describes export opportunities for U.S. business in more than 120 countries. Direct sales leads and names of companies and buyers are provided.

Time span: 1976–present. Updated quarterly.
Number of records: 57,700.
Available through: LIS.

Trade Opportunities Weekly This data base is a weekly update of *Trade Opportunities,* described above. Approximately 350 citations are added each week.

Time span: Current quarter. Updated weekly.
Number of records: 7,800.
Available through: LIS.

U.S. Exports Prepared by the U.S. Bureau of the Census from Shipper's Export Declarations, this data base provides export statistics covering both the private and public sectors of the United States and its territories.

> Time span: Current. Updated annually.
> Number of records: 150,000.
> Available through: LIS.

SCIENTIFIC AND TECHNICAL BREAKTHROUGHS

Agricola This comprehensive file of worldwide information on agriculture and related topics is produced by the National Agricultural Library of the Department of Agriculture. United States government reports, foreign- and domestic-journal articles, and monographs are included.

> Time span: 1970–present. Updated monthly.
> Number of records: 1,340,000.
> Available through: BRS; LIS; SDC.

APILIT International coverage of refining literature from journals, trade magazines, government reports, and conference papers can be found in this data base. Prepared by the Central Abstracting and Indexing Service of the American Petroleum Institute, such related areas as air and water conservation, storage and transportation, and petrochemicals are included.

> Time span: 1964–present. Updated monthly.
> Number of records: 18,000.
> Available through: SDC.

APIPAT Information on refining patents from the United States, Belgium, Canada, France, West Germany, Great Britain, Holland, Italy, Japan, and South Africa appear here. The Central Abstracting and Indexing Service of the American Petroleum Institute produces this data base.

> Time span: 1964–present. Updated monthly.
> Number of records: 110,000.
> Available through: SDC.

BIOSIS All aspects of the life sciences from around the world are covered in this data base, which abstracts nearly 8,000 primary journals as well as government reports, conference papers, preliminary reports, and reviews.

Time span: 1969–present. Updated monthly.
Number of records: 2,600,000.
Available through: BRS; LIS; SDC.

Chemical Abstracts Condensates The chemical sciences literature is covered in this data base produced by Chemical Abstract Services of the American Chemical Association. More than 12,000 journals, as well as books, reports, and proceedings, provide the basic input. Molecular formula fragment, registry numbers, and specific compounds can be searched on this comprehensive data base.

Time span: 1967–present. Updated biweekly.
Number of records: 4,362,000.
Available through: BRS; LIS; SDC.

CLAIMS™/U.S. Patent Abstracts If you are trying to locate a recent U.S. patent in the fields of science and technology, this data base will provide both citations and abstracts.

Time span: 1978–present. Updated monthly.
Number of records: 116,000.
Available through: LIS.

COMPENDEX This data base is the *Engineering Index's* worldwide coverage of the engineering and technology literature from about 3,500 journals and engineering societies' publications, as well as from proceedings, monographs, books, and government reports.

Time span: 1970–present. Updated monthly.
Number of records: 817,000.
Available through: LIS; SDC.

Conference Papers Index   Scientific and technical papers presented at more than 1,000 significant conferences each year can be located in this data base produced by Data Courier. Preprints, reprints, and abstracts are also included, as well as ordering information and costs.

> Time span: 1973–present. Updated monthly.
> Number of records: 715,000.
> Available through: LIS; SDC.

Current Research Information System   Current research in agriculture and related areas can be accessed in this data base produced by the United States Department of Agriculture Cooperative State Research Service.

> Time span: 1974–present. Updated quarterly.
> Number of records: 33,000.
> Available through: LIS.

Energyline   This data base provides information on all aspects of energy: technical, political, social, and economic. More than 200 journals are indexed in detail, 2,000 other publications are reviewed for energy issues, and applicable proceedings and reports are included.

> Time span: 1971–present. Updated bimonthly.
> Number of records: 29,000.
> Available through: LIS; SDC.

Enviroline   Worldwide coverage of environmental information can be found in this data base produced by Environment Information Center. More than 5,000 sources are reviewed for indexing and abstracting.

> Time span: 1971–present. Updated monthly.
> Number of records: 79,000.
> Available through: LIS; SDC.

INSPEC   This machine-readable version of *Physics Abstracts, Electrical and Electronic Abstracts,* and *Computer and Control Abstracts* is produced by The Institution of Electrical Engineers based in London, England. Source documents are international in scope and include approximately 2,000 journals.

> Time span: 1969–present. Updated monthly.
> Number of records: 1,404,000.
> Available through: BRS; LIS; SDC.

ISMEC   Information on mechanical engineering can be accessed through this data base produced by Data Courier, Inc. Worldwide coverage of the field includes both technical and management aspects.

> Time span: 1973–present. Updated monthly.
> Number of records: 98,000.
> Available through: LIS; SDC.

METADEX   The field of metallurgy is covered completely in this international data base, which is jointly produced by the American Society for Metals and the Metals Society located in London, England.

> Time span: 1966–present. Updated monthly.
> Number of records: 374,000.
> Available through: LIS.

NTIS   All unclassified, unlimited U.S. government-sponsored research and development by both private and public sector organizations is included in this data base produced by the National Technical Information Service. Reports can be ordered in hard copy or microfiche formats directly from NTIS.

> Time span: 1964–present. Updated biweekly.
> Number of records: 765,000.
> Available through: BRS; LIS; SDC.

Oceanic Abstracts   Marine information, such as oceanography, ships and shipping, and marine biology, can be found in this data base produced by Data Courier.

>   Time span: 1964–present. Updated bimonthly.
>   Number of records: 110,500.
>   Available through: LIS; SDC.

Pollution Abstracts   Pollution control; air, noise, and water pollution; solid wastes; and environmental quality are indicative of the kinds of information you can access through this data base.

>   Time span: 1970–present. Updated bimonthly.
>   Number of records: 68,500.
>   Available through: BRS; LIS; SDC.

SCISEARCH   Worldwide coverage of all fields of science and technology results in abstracts of 90 percent of all major technical literature being incorporated in this data base. A unique feature is citation indexing wherein all references cited by an author are linked to the article. Thus, searching for an older article that has been cited in a new technical paper will reveal the existence of this later published paper.

>   Time span: 1974–present. Updated monthly.
>   Number of records: 2,970,000.
>   Available through: LIS.

SPIN   This data base covers the world's literature on physics. Produced by the American Institute of Physics, the abstracts are prepared by the original authors.

>   Time span: 1975–present. Updated monthly.
>   Number of records: 114,000.
>   Available through: LIS.

SSIE   If you want to know about recently completed and current research, even before the information appears in reports or professional journals, this data base will provide that information.

Produced by the Smithsonian Science Information Exchange, both public and private sector research is included.

Time span: Past two years to the present. Updated monthly.
Number of records: 299,000.
Available through: BRS; LIS; SDC.

TRIS Transportation Research Information Service, produced by the U.S. Department of Transportation and the Transportation Research Board, provides information on highway, rail, air, and sea transportation modes. Urban mass transportation, traffic control and communication, and safety exemplify the subjects covered.

Time span: 1968–present. Updated monthly.
Number of records: 145,000.
Available through: LIS.

WPI World Patent Index, prepared by Derwent Publications, Ltd., London, England, covers patent specifications from the Patent Offices of the industrialized nations.

Time span: 1963–present. Updated monthly.
Number of records: 1,000,000.
Available through: SDC.

SPECIAL SOURCES OF INFORMATION

ASI American Statistics Index provides an in-depth indexing and abstract of U.S. government statistical publications. Social, economic, and demographic data from more than 400 government agencies are covered.

Time span: 1973–present. Updated monthly.
Number of records: 55,000.
Available through: LIS; SDC.

CIS Index Published by Congressional Information Service, this data base indexes publications of the United States Congress. Hearings, reports, documents, and special publications (including testimony from private and public witnesses) are covered.

Time span: 1970–present. Updated monthly.
Number of records: 110,000.
Available through: LIS; SDC.

CRECORD   This data base provides comprehensive coverage
of the *Congressional Record.* References are indexed to 275 legislative areas.

Time span: 1976–present. Updated weekly.
Number of records: 180,000.
Available through: LIS; SDC.

Dow Jones News/Retrieval Service   This is a full-text data base
that covers business, economic, and management information from
The Wall Street Journal, Barron's Weekly, and the Dow Jones
Broad Tape Service as well as such items as company news.

Time span: Preceding 90 days to the present. Updated daily.
Number of records: 6,000.
Available through:
   Dow Jones & Company, Inc.
   22 Cortlandt Street
   New York,NY 10007
   (800) 257-5114

Encyclopedia of Associations   Information on several thousand
trade and professional organizations can be accessed on this data
base, which provides addresses, phone numbers, lists of publications, dates and places of annual conferences, and sizes of organizations.

Time span: Current year. Updated annually.
Number of records: 14,000.
Available through: LIS.

Federal Register   Abstracts of the rules, regulations, public law
notices, and proposed rules by the federal government that appear
daily in the *Federal Register* are covered by this data base.

Time span: 1977–present. Updated weekly.
Number of records: 54,000.
Available through: LIS.

Foundation Directory About 3,200 foundations that make annual grants of more than $100,000 or whose assets exceed $1,000,000 are described in this directory produced by The Foundation Center.

Time span: Current year. Updated semiannually.
Number of records: 3,200.
Available through: LIS.

GPO Monthly Catalog Publications of the U.S. Government Printing Office are listed here. The information ranges from fact sheets and maps to handbooks and reports and includes congressional hearings.

Time span: 1976–present. Updated monthly.
Number of records: 75,000.
Available through: BRS; LIS.

The Information Bank Prepared by the New York Times Information Bank, this data base provides citations and abstracts from *The New York Times* as well as material from 70 other newspapers and journals. Business news is covered in depth.

Time span: 1969–present. Updated daily.
Number of records: 2,500,000.
Available through:
New York Times Information Service
1719A Route 10
Parsippany, NJ 07054
(201) 539-5850

National Foundations United States foundations that provide grants of any amount are listed in this directory. About 17,000 foundations (many restricting their donations regionally or locally) that are not included in the *Foundation Directory* are covered here.

Time span: Current year. Updated annually.
Number of records: 21,800.
Available through: LIS.

National Newspaper Index   This data base provides complete indexing of *The Christian Science Monitor, The New York Times,* and *The Wall Street Journal,* and includes illustrations, cartoons, and letters to the editor. Crossword puzzles, horoscopes, stock market tables, and weather charts are the only material not included.

Time span: 1979–present. Updated monthly.
Number of records: 165,000.
Available through: LIS.

Newsearch   Nearly 400 newspapers, periodicals, and magazines are indexed to provide information on news stories, book reviews, and general information articles.

Time span: Current month. Updated daily.
Number of records: 1,500.
Available through: LIS.

PAIS International   All public policy issues are referenced in this data base, which has worldwide coverage. Prepared by the Public Affairs Information Service, more than 800 journals and 6,000 individual publications are indexed.

Time span: 1972–present. Updated quarterly.
Number of records: 107,000.
Available through: BRS; LIS.

B

INFORMATION FOR A FEE—
A SELECTED LIST OF INFORMATION
BROKERS

Bogart-Brociner Associates, Inc.
47 Williams Drive
Annapolis, MD 21401
DC area: (301) 261-2893
MD area: (301) 267-8354

Chase World Information Corporation
One World Trade Center, Suite 7800
New York, NY 10048
(212) 432-8000

Colorado Technical Reference Center
Campus Box 184, Norlin Library

University of Colorado
Boulder, CO 80309
(303) 492-8774

Computer Search Center
Illinois Institute of Technology Research
10 West 35th Street
Chicago, IL 60616
(312) 567-4341

Dataque International, Inc.
John Hancock Center
875 North Michigan Avenue, Suite 3430
Chicago, IL 60611
(312) 951-5351

Documentation Associates
1513 Sixth Street, Suite 104A
Santa Monica, CA 90401
(213) 477-5081

Facts for a Fee
Cleveland Public Library
325 Superior Avenue
Cleveland, OH 44114
(216) 623-2999

Find/SVP
500 Fifth Avenue
New York, NY 10110
(212) 354-2424

FOI Services, Inc.
12315 Wilkins Avenue
Rockville, MD 20852
(301) 881-0410

Franklin Institute Research
    Laboratories
Science Information Service
    Department
20th Street and Benjamin
    Franklin Parkway
Philadelphia, PA 19103
(215) 448-1227

Inform
Minneapolis Public Library
    and Information Center
300 Nicollet Mall
Minneapolis, MN 55401
(612) 372-6636

The Info-Mart
P.O. Box 2400
Santa Barbara, CA 93120
(805) 965-5555

Information for Business
25 West 39th Street
New York, NY 10018
(212) 840-1220

50 Church Street
Cambridge, MA 02138
(617) 876-7776

Information Management Spe-
    cialists
1816 Race Street
Denver, CO 80206
(303) 320-0116

Information On Demand
P.O. Box 4536
2511 Channing Way, Suite B
Berkeley, CA 94704
(415) 841-1145

The Information Store
235 Montgomery Street,
    Suite 800
San Francisco, CA 94104
(415) 421-9376

Arthur D. Little, Inc.
25 Acorn Park
Cambridge, MA 02140
(617) 864-5770

Massachusetts Institute of
    Technology Libraries
Computerized Literature
    Search Service
Room 14S-M48
77 Massachusetts Avenue
Cambridge, MA 02139
(617) 253-7746

NASA Industrial Applications
Center
LIS Building
University of Pittsburgh
Pittsburgh, PA 15260
(412) 624-5213

National Investment Library
80 Wall Street
New York, NY 10005
(212) 982-2000
(800) 221-5644

New England Research Applications Center (NERAC)
University of Connecticut
Mansfield Professional Park
Storrs, CT 06268
(203) 486-4533

Packaged Facts, Inc.
274 Madison Avenue
New York, NY 10016
(212) 532-5533

Regional Information & Communication Exchange
Fondren Library
Rice University
Box 1892
Houston, TX 77001
(713) 528-3553

Roberts Information Services, Inc. (ROBINS)
8306 Hilltop Road
Fairfax, VA 22031
(703) 560-7888

Warner-Eddison Associates, Inc.
186 Alewife Brook Parkway
Cambridge, MA 02138
(617) 661-8124

Washington Researchers
918 16th Street, NW
Washington, DC 20006
(202) 833-2230

Washington Service Bureau, Inc.
1225 Connecticut Avenue, NW, Suite 600
Washington, DC 20036
(202) 833-9200

World Trade Information Center
One World Trade Center, Suite 86001
New York, NY 10048
(212) 466-3063

World Trade Library and Business Information Center of Golden Gate University
536 Mission Street, Room 549
San Francisco, CA 94105
(415) 442-7244

World Wide Information Services, Inc.
660 First Avenue
New York, NY 10016
(212) 679-7240

C

INFORMATION FOR "FREE"—
A SELECTED DIRECTORY OF
FEDERAL INFORMATION RESOURCES

Managers interested in information on various activities, programs, and services of the federal government may visit, phone, or write the Federal Information Centers for assistance in locating the government agency which has that information. The General Services Administration maintains these information centers throughout the United States. The following is a directory of the centers with tieline numbers.

State/City	Telephone*	Address	Toll-Free Tieline to
ALABAMA:			
Birmingham	322-8591		Atlanta, GA
Mobile	438-1421		New Orleans, LA
ALASKA: Anchorage	907-271-3650	Federal Bldg.–U.S. Courthouse, 701 C St., 99513.	
ARIZONA:			
Tucson	622-1511		Phoenix, AZ
Phoenix	602-261-3313	Federal Bldg., 230 N. 1st Ave., 85025.	
ARKANSAS: Little Rock	378-6177		Memphis, TN
CALIFORNIA:			
Los Angeles	213-688-3800	Federal Bldg., 300 N. Los Angeles St., 90012.	
Sacramento	916-440-3344	Federal Bldg.–U.S. Courthouse, 650 Capitol Mall, 95814.	
San Diego	714-293-6030	Government Info. Center, Federal Bldg., 880 Front St., 92188.	
San Francisco	415-556-6600	Federal Bldg.–U.S. Courthouse, 450 Golden Gate Ave., 94102.	
San Jose	275-7422		San Francisco, CA
Santa Ana	836-2386		Los Angeles, CA
COLORADO:			
Colorado Springs	471-9491		Denver, CO
Denver	303-837-3602	Federal Bldg., 1961 Stout St., 80294.	
Pueblo	544-9523		Denver, CO

* The tieline numbers are toll-free only in the specified city.

State/City	Telephone*	Address	Toll-Free Tieline to
CONNECTICUT:			
Hartford	527-2617		New York, NY
New Haven	624-4720		New York, NY
DISTRICT OF COLUMBIA	202-755-8660	7th and D Sts. S.W., 20407.	
FLORIDA:			
Fort Lauderdale	522-8531		Miami, FL
Jacksonville	354-4756		St. Petersburg, FL
Miami	305-350-4155	Federal Bldg., 51 S.W. 1st Ave., 33130.	
Orlando	422-1800		St. Petersburg, FL
St. Petersburg	813-893-3495	Cramer Federal Bldg., 144 1st Ave. S., 33701.	
Tampa	229-7911		St. Petersburg, FL
West Palm Beach	833-7566		Miami, FL
Other south Florida locations	800-432-6668		Miami, FL
Other north Florida locations	800-282-8556		St. Petersburg, FL
GEORGIA: Atlanta	404-221-6891	Russell Federal Bldg.–U.S. Courthouse, 75 Spring St. S.W., 30303.	
HAWAII: Honolulu	808-546-8620	300 Ala Moana Blvd., 96850.	
ILLINOIS: Chicago	312-353-4242	Everett McKinley Dirksen Bldg., Room 250, 219 S. Dearborn St., 60604.	
INDIANA:			
Gary	883-4110		
Indianapolis	317-269-7373	Federal Bldg., 575 N. Pennsylvania St., 46204.	Indianapolis, IN

IOWA:

Des Moines — 515-284-4448 — Federal Bldg., 210 Walnut St., 50309. — Des Moines, IA

Other Iowa locations — 800-532-1556

KANSAS:

Topeka — 913-295-2866 — Federal Bldg.–U.S. Courthouse, 444 S.E. Quincy, 66683.

Other Kansas locations — 800-432-2934 — Federal Bldg., 600 Federal Place, 40202. — Kansas City, MO

KENTUCKY: Louisville — 502-582-6261

LOUISIANA: New Orleans — 504-589-6696 — , U.S. Postal Service Bldg., 701 Loyola Ave., 70113.

MARYLAND: Baltimore — 301-962-4980 — Federal Bldg., 31 Hopkins Plaza, 21201.

MASSACHUSETTS: Boston — 617-223-7121 — John F. Kennedy Federal Bldg., Room E-130, Cambridge St., 02203.

MICHIGAN:

Detroit — 313-226-7016 — McNamara Federal Bldg., 477 Michigan Ave., 48226. — Detroit, MI

Grand Rapids — 451-2628

MINNESOTA: Minneapolis — 612-725-2073 — Federal Bldg.–U.S. Courthouse, 110 S. 4th St., 55401.

MISSOURI:

Kansas City — 816-374-2466 — Federal Bldg., 601 E. 12th St., 64106.

St. Louis — 314-425-4106 — Federal Bldg., 1520 Market St., 63103.

State/City	Telephone*	Address	Toll-Free Tieline to
Other Missouri locations within area code 314.	800-392-7711		St. Louis, MO
Other Missouri locations within area codes 816 and 417.	800-892-5808		Kansas City, MO
NEBRASKA:			
Omaha	402-221-3353	U.S. Post Office and Courthouse, 215 N. 17th St., 68102.	
Other Nebraska Locations	800-642-8383		Omaha, NE
NEW JERSEY:			
Newark	201-645-3600	Federal Bldg., 970 Broad St., 07102.	
Paterson/Passaic	523-0717		Newark, NJ
Trenton	396-4400		Newark, NJ
NEW MEXICO:			
Albuquerque	505-766-3091	Federal Bldg.–U.S. Courthouse, 500 Gold Ave. S.W., 87102.	
Santa Fe	983-7743		Albuquerque, NM
NEW YORK:			
Albany	463-4421		New York, NY
Buffalo	716-846-4010	Federal Bldg., 111 W. Huron St., 14202.	
New York	212-264-4464	Federal Office Bldg., 26 Federal Plaza, 10007.	
Rochester	546-5075		Buffalo, NY.
Syracuse	476-8545		Buffalo, NY

NORTH CAROLINA:			
Charlotte	376-3600		Atlanta, GA
OHIO:			
Akron	375-5638		Cleveland, OH
Cincinnati	513-684-2801	Federal Bldg., 550 Main St., 45202.	
Cleveland	216-522-4040	Federal Bldg., 1240 E. 9th St., 44199.	
Columbus	221-1014		Cincinnati, OH
Dayton	223-7377		Cincinnati, OH
Toledo	241-3223		Cleveland, OH
OKLAHOMA:			
Oklahoma City	405-231-4868	U.S. Post Office and Courthouse, 201 N.W. 3d St., 73102.	Oklahoma City, OK
Tulsa	584-4193		
OREGON: Portland	503-221-2222	Federal Bldg., Room 109, 1220 S.W. 3d Ave., 97204.	
PENNSYLVANIA:			
Philadelphia	215-597-7042	William J. Green, Jr. Federal Bldg., 600 Arch St., 19106.	Philadelphia, PA
Allentown/Bethlehem	821-7785		
Pittsburgh	412-644-3456	Federal Bldg., 1000 Liberty Ave., 15222.	
Scranton	346-7081		Philadelphia, PA
RHODE ISLAND: Providence	331-5565		Boston, MA

State/City	Telephone*	Address	Toll-Free Tieline to
TENNESSEE:			
Chattanooga	265-8231		Memphis, TN
Memphis	901-521-3285	Clifford Davis Federal Bldg., 167 N. Main St., 38103.	
Nashville	242-5056		Memphis, TN
TEXAS:			
Austin	472-5494		Houston, TX
Dallas	767-8585		Fort Worth, TX
Fort Worth	817-334-3624	Fritz Garland Lanham Federal Bldg., 819 Taylor St., 76102.	
Houston	713-226-5711	Federal Bldg.–U.S. Courthouse, 515 Rusk Ave., 77208.	
San Antonio	224-4471		Houston, TX
UTAH:			
Ogden	399-1347		Salt Lake City, UT
Salt Lake City	801-524-5353	Federal Bldg., Room 1205, 125 S. State St., 84138.	
VIRGINIA:			
Newport News	244-0480		Norfolk, VA
Norfolk	804-441-3101	Federal Bldg., 200 Granby Mall, Room 120, 23510.	
Richmond	643-4928		Norfolk, VA
Roanoke	982-8591		Norfolk, VA
WASHINGTON:			
Seattle	206-442-0570	Federal Bldg., 915 2d Ave., 98174.	Seattle, WA
Tacoma	383-5230		
WISCONSIN: Milwaukee	271-2273		Chicago, IL

FEDERAL PUBLICATIONS

If you are interested in locating a publication printed by the Government Printing Office (GPO), dial (202) 783-3238. Once GPO has identified the correct title and stock number, you can place your order immediately and charge it to your Master Card or Visa account. Or you may send a check or money order payable to the Superintendent of Documents, U.S. Government Printing Office, Washington, DC 20402. Frequently your congressman's office can obtain the document for you at no cost. Also, many government publications are available to you in federal depository libraries throughout the country. To find your nearest depository library call a Federal Information Center listed above or your local library.

REFERRAL SERVICE

The Library of Congress maintains a National Referral Center that can refer you to individuals and organizations, both public and private, to help answer your questions. Its number is (202) 287-5670.

FEDERAL LEGISLATION

Copies of bills passed by the House or Senate may be obtained free of charge from the respective document rooms. Complete titles and numbers may be obtained by calling the following telephone numbers, but requests must be made in writing or in person.

House Document Room
U.S. Capitol Building, Room H-226
Washington, DC 20515
(202) 225-3456
Senate Document Room
U.S. Capitol Building, Room S-325
Washington, DC 20510
(202) 224-4321

If you want to know the status of a bill, dial (202) 225-1772.

SMALL-BUSINESS INFORMATION

Dial (202) 653-6979 for information pertaining to small businesses.

D

SELECTED BIBLIOGRAPHY
WITH NOTES AND EXCERPTS

THE AGE OF INFORMATION

Bell, Daniel. *The Coming of Post-Industrial Society.* New York: Basic Books, 1973.

Bell coined the term post-industrial society. He defines the phrase in this classic work. "The post-industrial society, it is clear, is a knowledge society in a double sense: first, the sources of innovation are increasingly derivative from research and development (and more directly, there is a new relation between science and technology because of the centrality of *theoretical* knowledge); second, the weight of society—measured by a larger proportion of Gross National Product and a larger share of employment—is increasingly in the knowledge field."

Kahn, Herman, and Phelps, John B. "The Economic Present and Future." *The Futurist,* June 1979, pp. 202–222.

Kahn and his staff at the Hudson Institute present a broadly optimistic view of the next 20 years through a series of 26 charts that are analytic summaries of the text. The authors state, "We have noted that humanity is gradually entering a new state of development called the post-industrial society. The transition to this state is causing serious stresses, which are the subject of so much controversy."

Porat, Marc Uri. *The Information Economy.* U.S. Department of Commerce. Office of Telecommunications. OT Special Publication 77-12. Washington, D.C.: Government Printing Office, 1977.

This nine-volume publication measures information's place in today's economy. Volumes 1 and 2 are the most critical part of the whole series. The other volumes are essentially supplemental. Volume 1 contains the study's major findings. It provides a comprehensive definition of information activity, breaking this down into primary and secondary sectors. Volume 2 discusses the 25 major industries that compose the primary information sector.

Withington, Frederic G. "Transformation of the Information Industries." *Datamation,* November 1978, pp. 8–14.

The author reviews ". . . the basic structural forces shaping the information industries." Although the results of this transformation are uncertain, he concludes that ". . . an individual firm which provides or uses the product of the information industries can plan rationally."

MOTIVATION, PRODUCTIVITY, POWER

Herzberg, Frederick. "Herzberg on Motivation for the '80s." *Industry Week,* October 1, 1979, pp. 58–63.

Herzberg contends that today's manager must face a confused mixture of value systems developed in the 1970s by a labor force comprised of pre-World War II, 1950, and 1960 workers. He proposes that "a sound labor philosophy for the eighties must rest on the basic need of human beings to be needed. People want to be responsible and efficient when they can perceive that their work serves a meaningful purpose."

Improving Productivity: A Self-Audit and Guide for Federal Executives and Managers. National Center for Productivity and Quality of Working Life. Washington, D.C.: Government Printing Office, Fall 1978.

"This report describes the components of a continuing, organized productivity improvement effort which should involve all levels of management and personnel." Many of the suggestions are applicable to private-sector managers.

Kanter, Rosabeth Moss. "Power Failure in Management Circuits." *Harvard Business Review,* July–August 1979, pp. 65–75.

Kanter declares, "Lacking the supplies, information, or support to make things happen easily, they [the powerless] may turn instead to the ultimate weapon of those who lack productive power—oppressive power: holding others back and punishing with whatever threats they can muster." She describes three positions that are susceptible to powerlessness: first-line supervisors, staff professionals, and top executives. She suggests that sharing power can increase organizational power.

Miller, Donald B. "How to Improve the Performance and Productivity of the Knowledge Worker." *Organizational Dynamics*, 5:3 (Winter 1977), pp. 62–80.

The author's theme, that "improvement in engineering productivity and improvement in the quality of working life for engineers are positively correlated," is based on his experiences at IBM in San Jose. He proposes four concepts to improve the quality of working life: ". . . raise the value and priority of continued learning, growth, and personal vitality in the work environment . . . provide a better growth environment . . . define professional productivity . . . encourage engineers to increase their self-understanding."

Spencer, William I. "What Do Upper Executives Want from MIS?" *Administrative Management*, July 1978, pp. 26–27, 66, 68. Copyright © 1978 by Geyer-McAllister Publications, Inc., New York.

The author, president of Citicorp, New York, answers the title's question by saying, "All that top management wants from the management information system is exactly enough of the most relevant information at precisely the right moment to produce an infallible management decision—and, of course, at the least possible cost."

Yankelovich, Daniel. "Yankelovich on Today's Workers: We Need New Motivational Tools." *Industry Week*, August 6, 1979, pp. 61–68.

This expert on motivation states that the traditional incentives of fear, money, work organization, and the work ethic have become blunted as motivational tools. He describes ". . . areas from which the incentives of the future are going to come, or be shaped: . . . innovative and ingenious ways of using time . . . leisure and health opportunities . . . customized feedback mechanisms on achievement . . . greater distribution of amenities . . . providing the opportunity to practice one's life-style, or at least to symbolize it in relationship to work."

INFORMATION TECHNOLOGY

Anderson, Howard. "Electronic Mail of the '80s." *The Office,* November 1979, pp. 18–22.

The author, president of The Yankee Group, Cambridge, Massachusetts, offers an 11-point plan to determine if electronic mail is worthwhile for your company. "Electronic mail offers a variety of advantages and some very severe traps for the novice user. A systematic method of evaluation and approach will allow the user to access the advantages while avoiding the traps."

Connell, John J. "Office of the 80s." Special Advertising Section, *Business Week,* February 18, 1980, pp. 20–52.

Connell offers the reader seven productivity strategies with the ultimate result of expanding human potential. "This special supplement addresses the problems and the potential of the Office of the 80s. It describes why office costs are rising; proposes that increasing office worker productivity at all levels should be a key managerial objective; describes approaches, tools and techniques for achieving that objective; and discusses the opportunities and the pitfalls in managing the move into the Office of the Future."

Drucker, Peter F. "Managing the Information Explosion." *The Wall Street Journal,* April 10, 1980, p. 24.

According to Drucker, "The greatest impact of the new information technology . . . will not be on the human organization but on the production process." He labels this integration of information processing and production in machines and tools as the "third industrial revolution."

Johansen, Robert; Vallee, Jacques; and Spangler, Kathleen. "Electronic Meetings: Utopian Dreams and Complex Realities." *The Futurist,* October 1978, pp. 313–318.

The authors describe the three alternatives to face-to-face meetings: video, computer, and audio teleconferencing. "Teleconferencing media do indeed offer real opportunities to improve communication by reducing the barriers of space and time." But they also caution that teleconferencing ". . . does not eliminate the possibility of ineffective meetings. Instead, it changes the nature of meetings in ways which increase the possibilities for both good and bad outcomes."

Miller, William H. "Taming the Information Monster." *Industry Week,* January 7, 1980, pp. 55–60.
Miller discusses the convergence of technologies in computers, communications, and office automation. "Conveniently, the confluence of technologies comes at a time when industry's need for information is greater than ever. . . . But the greatest opportunity of all for the converging technologies might be to help U.S. industry combat what is often regarded as its greatest problem: sagging productivity growth."

Prince, Jeffrey S. "Conference Systems in the 80s." *Administrative Management,* April 1980, pp. 65–66, 70, 74. Copyright © 1980 by Geyer-McAllister Publications, Inc., New York.
"Whether computer terminals, phone lines, or video linkups are employed, administrative managers, however, will be attracted by the more productive use of time, reduced travel, and the ability to participate in meetings in different cities on the same day."

INFORMATION SOURCES

Darrow, Joel W., and Belilove, James R. "The Growth of Databank Sharing." *Harvard Business Review,* November–December 1978, pp. 180–194.
This thorough article covers the information that can be shared, make-or-buy decisions, cost of databanks, structure of the industry, and examples of databank products available in ten subjects areas. The authors stated, "Although learning what databanks are available is not too difficult, deciding which to acquire and how to use them can be far more complicated. Using these products, managers can improve any organization, but they will need to avoid the pitfalls, which stem from their lack of experience in the sharing process."

Kiechel, III, Walter. "Everything You Always Wanted to Know May Soon Be On-Line." *Fortune,* May 5, 1980, pp. 226–240. Copyright © 1980 Time, Inc. All Rights Reserved.
Kiechel looks at the business of collecting, packaging, and distributing information in on-line data bases. "What the new businesses provide is not so much additional information . . . but a radical improvement in the ease with which information can be retrieved, a promise that the curious can find what they need to know in just a matter of seconds."

Washington Researchers. *How to Find Information About Companies.*
Washington, D.C.: Washington Researchers, 1979.
This is a helpful guide to locate information about domestic and foreign
companies. Sources include local, state, and federal government, the
courts, and private sector resources such as trade associations and labor
unions, investigative services, credit-reporting and bond-rating services,
and organizations that provide information services.

INFORMATION AS A RESOURCE

"Diebold Special Report Part 1; Information Resource Management—the
New Challenge." *Infosystems,* June 1979, pp. 50–92.
This special series of seven articles compiled by The Diebold Group,
Inc., management consultants, deals with planning information technology for the next decade. John Diebold, Chairman, The Diebold
Group, Inc., begins ". . . by providing an executive overview of the role
of information management in the 1980s, a role that will change in
many fundamental ways. Among the areas that will undergo alteration
and that can be anticipated and planned for are the information manager's span of control, the proliferation of computer hardware, and the
expanded range of decision-making and business transactions within
the guidelines of corporate information management."

"Diebold Special Report Part 2; Information Resource Management: New
Directions in Management." *Infosystems,* October 1979, pp. 41–120.
Eleven articles compose this second installment on information resource management. John Diebold, Chairman, The Diebold Group,
Inc., sets the tone in his foreword. "Information, which in essence is the
analysis and synthesis of data, will unquestionably be one of the most
vital of corporate resources in the 1980s. It will be structured into
models for planning and decision making. It will be incorporated into
measurements of performance and profitability. It will be integrated
into product design and marketing methods. In other words, information will be recognized and treated as an asset."

Lieberstein, Stanley H. *Who Own What Is in Your Head? Trade Secrets and
the Mobile Employee.* New York: Hawthorn Books, 1979.
This is a lawyer's view of the conflict of employees' rights of mobility
and the needs of company confidentiality. He addresses those aspects of
". . . employer–employee relationships that involve: 1. trade secrets, be
they of a business nature—personal business relationships, including

valuable customer lists and client contacts developed through the auspices of an employer—or of a technical nature, *i.e.,* relating to manufacturing processes; 2. ideas, patentable or not, created in whole or in part by the employee."

Parker, Royal. "Handling Transborder Data Flow—A Global Concern." *Financial Executive,* December 1979, pp. 38–46.

According to Parker, "Transborder information flow . . . deals with the movement of data across international borders . . . and it covers the interrelated issues of privacy, national security, economics, protectionism, and national cultural independence. . . . But, it is extremely important that the business community remain alert to these developments and engage in ongoing public debate to ensure that there are no adverse impacts on the international economic system."

Porat, Marc Uri. "Global Implications of the Information Society." *Journal of Communication,* 28:1 (Winter 1978), pp. 70–79.

Porat forecasts a bright future in an information society, if intelligent information policies are formulated. He calls for the resolution of such social and economic domestic issues as ". . . contradictions between the Privacy Act and the Freedom of Information Act; First Amendment issues and the bounds of commercial speech; the federal paperwork burden; the Copyright Act. . . . Domestic policy will also focus on the structure of the information industry. . . . And finally, attention will necessarily focus on the international implications—the exports of information goods and services, cultural exports, and technological and scientific information transfer."

Read, William H. "Information as a National Resource." *Journal of Communication,* 29:1 (Winter 1979), pp. 172–178.

Read feels that "For the makers of foreign policy, the fact that information can be viewed in resource terms should be a welcome one. A policy planner can begin work by asking a standard set of questions. Who has the resource? Who wants the resource? And what are the terms of exchange?"

Zurkowski, Paul G. "Misconceptions About Information Are Costing the United States a Bundle." *Publishers Weekly,* June 9, 1979, pp. 37–38. Excerpt reprinted from *Publishers Weekly,* June 9, 1979, published by the R. R. Bowker Company, a Xerox company. © 1979 Xerox Corporation.

Zurkowski, president of Information Industry Association, states, "In our own national interest, the logical extension of the proposition that information is a national resource must be built into our overall national and international policies. These matters are of immediate and substantial concern."

PLANNING, BUDGETING, AUDITING

Drinan, Helen. "Financial Management of Online Services—A How-to Guide." *Online,* October 1979, pp. 14–21.

Drinan reports, "The decision to alter the financial management of online services from partial to total cost recovery mandated an examination of service associated costs that was more detailed than previous budget objectives had required. This process resulted in a methodology which can be used as a model for the cost-recovery based financial management of online services in any information center. This methodology is premised on a break-even analysis, one which attempts to balance expenses and user charges, with no provision for profit. It encompasses three major financial tasks: budgeting, pricing and controlling."

Horton, Jr., Forest Woody. "Budgeting and Accounting for Information." *The Government Accountant's Journal,* 28:1 (Spring 1979), pp. 21–31.

Horton's thesis is: "The cost of information can be made visible and categorized in two ways, by the development and use of an *Information Object Classification* and by focusing on how information is actually used, the Information System of an organization."

"The New Planning." *Business Week,* December 18, 1978, pp. 62–68.

According to this article, ". . . the role of the CEO as entrepreneur is being replaced by his role as ringmaster, while the line manager's traditional role of implementer and conservator is being reversed to that of entrepreneur. . . . Problems can arise with computer-based planning if executives do not have a clear idea of the kind of information they want to get out of the computer."

Quinn, Anne V. "The Information Audit." *The Information Manager,* May–June 1979, pp. 18–19.

The author, an Arthur D. Little consultant, provides a seven-element profile that should be constructed for every information center in a company. "The auditor's task then is to integrate the data gathered from all of the information profiles, indicate where the information systems fall short, and help fomulate goals and recommendations for the new 'ideal' information center."

Rockart, John F. "Chief Executives Define Their Own Data Needs." *Harvard Business Review,* March–April 1979, pp. 81–93.

Rockart states, "The MIT research team's experience in the past two years with the critical success factors (CSF) approach suggests that it is highly effective in helping executives to define their significant information needs.... Every chief executive appears to have, at some level, both monitoring and building (or adapting) responsibilities. Thus a great deal of the information needed will not continue to be needed year after year. Rather, it is relatively short-term 'project status' information that is needed only during the project's lifetime. Periodic review of CSFs will therefore bring to light the need to discontinue some reports and initiate others."

Strassmann, Paul A. "Managing the Costs of Information." *Harvard Business Review,* September–October 1976, pp. 133–142.

Strassmann offers a nine-step sequence to control information systems programs. "The sequence should start with the budgeting process. It must identify all of the components of information processing cost and segment them by (1) function ... (2) technology ... and (3) organization."

MANAGING INFORMATION

Buhler, Warren B. "All of Us Can Reduce Red Tape." *Across the Board,* September 1978, pp. 34–36.

This former director of the Commission on Federal Paperwork offers more than 40 ways to cut paperwork. He concludes, "... business should not accept all paperwork as inevitable. Instead, it must be prepared, with facts and a cooperative spirit, to help government find less expensive and more effective ways of achieving our national goals."

Commission on Federal Paperwork. *Reference Manual for Program and Information Officials.* Washington, D.C.: Government Printing Office, 1978.

Volume 1, *A Handbook for Managers,* covers in 69 pages information resources management, service management, the information resources management (IRM) function, managing information resources, and management responsibilities. Its purpose is to help federal agency program officials improve the quality and effectiveness of data collection and information resource utilization.

Volume 2, *A Handbook for Technical Information Personnel,* is more detailed. Its objective ". . . is to improve the quality and effectiveness of all the myriad activities involved in planning, managing and controlling data, information and paperwork." Subjects such as budgeting and measuring the IRM program, confidentiality and privacy, and safeguarding information are covered in the 340 pages. Both volumes provide information that is applicable to business and industry.

Kaufman, Herbert. *Red Tape. Its Origins, Uses, and Abuses.* Washington, D.C.: The Brookings Institution, 1977.

This senior fellow at the Brookings Institution declares, "Red tape has thus taken its place with death and taxes as an inevitability of life. It may even be more durable than they are."

Montgomery, David B., and Weinberg, Charles B. "Toward Strategic Intelligence Systems," *Journal of Marketing,* 43:4 (Fall 1979), pp. 41–52.

This article is the result of interviews with more than 100 executives in over 30 companies. According to the authors, "This paper is designed first to present an overview of strategic intelligence systems (SIS)—their purpose and the kinds of information they gather. The second section discusses the collection of strategic intelligence. The final section provides a brief discussion of the analysis and processing of strategic intelligence."

ORGANIZATIONAL STRUCTURE

Holmes, Fenwicke W. "IRM: Organizing for the Office of the Future." *Journal of Systems Management,* 43:1 (January 1979), pp. 24–31.

Holmes states, "It is still too early in the development of the automated or technological office of the future to propose an 'ideal' structure." He suggests that in the interim task forces be organized. "What you must do is to put people from diverse interests and areas of specialization into *ad hoc* groupings. Task forces can be powerful implements for change."

Pullen, Edward W., and Simko, Robert G. "Our Changing Industry." *Datamation,* January 1977, pp. 49–55.

The authors document the growth and expansion of the data processing market and the increase in technical innovations that are driving forces in changing the data processing systems business into an information systems business. "To deal with this environment, companies will need to develop some very different concepts and skills. Dp [data processing] management will be joined or eclipsed by: a corporate communications architect/administrator, an information inventory/resource manager, and a corporate teleprocessing/communications manager."

CAREER PLANNING

Connell, John J. "How Your Job Will Change in the Next 10 Years." *Administrative Management,* January 1979, pp. 26–28, 53. Copyright © 1979 by Geyer-McAllister Publications, Inc., New York.

This executive director of the Office Technology Research Group predicts, "Over the next decade, then, the administrative manager will be called upon to be a manager of technology, a manager of information, and a manager of people. In many cases, the assignment will grow in stature and the administrative manager will reach the ranks of senior management."

Horton, Jr., Forest W. *Information Resources Management: Concept and Cases.* Cleveland: Association for Systems Management, 1979.

This is the first textbook on information resources management. It contains discussion questions at the end of each chapter and provides cases to reinforce the concepts highlighted in the book. "Much of the work was drawn from the author's experience with the Commission on Federal Paperwork, which found that the paperwork burden on the American public was far more than a matter of physical pieces of paper, but, instead, had its roots in ineffective data and information policies of the Federal Government. Of necessity, then, examples and illustrations were drawn from government, but they have direct applicability to business, and more broadly, to the private sector."

FREEDOM OF INFORMATION AND PRIVACY

Montgomery, David B.; Peters, Anne H.; and Weinberg, Charles B. "The Freedom of Information Act: Strategic Opportunities and Threats." *Sloan Management Review,* 19:2 (Winter 1978), pp. 1–13. Excerpt reprinted by permission of the publisher. Copyright © 1978 by The Sloan Management Review Association. All Rights Reserved.

The authors present examples of how ". . . business has increasingly used the Act to obtain strategic intelligence from the Federal government relating to both competitors and government policy formulation processes." They suggest seven action implications of the Freedom of

Information Act for managers to consider from both offensive and defensive positions.

Privacy Protection Study Commission. *Personal Privacy in an Information Society.* Washington, D.C.: Government Printing Office, 1977.

The commission, under the chairmanship of David F. Linowes, spent two years examining individual privacy rights and record-keeping processes in many environments, with emphasis on the private sector. Consumer credit organizers, commercial banks and savings and loan institutions, insurance companies, the employer–employee relationship, investigative-reporting agencies were just some of the areas researched in this 654-page report. The commission ". . . concluded that an effective privacy protection policy must have three concurrent objectives: . . . to minimize intrusiveness . . . to maximize fairness . . . to create legitimate, enforceable expectations of confidentiality."

U.S. Congress, House of Representatives, Committee on Government Operations, *A Citizen's Guide on How to Use The Freedom of Information Act and The Privacy Act in Requesting Government Documents.* Union Calendar No. 412, Report No. 95–793. 95th Congress, 1st Session, Washington, D.C., 1977.

This 59-page report provides detailed information on how to use The Freedom of Information Act and The Privacy Act to obtain information. Sample request letters are included as well as fee schedules. Addresses of selected government agencies are listed in an appendix.

Westin, Alan F. "Message to CEOs—About Employee Privacy." *Across the Board,* June 1979, pp. 8–13.

According to Westin, "Employee privacy is one of the hottest items in corporate boardrooms these days." He reports what several pioneering companies have done in developing employee privacy policies. He concludes, "Whether voluntary programs will be given time to spread or whether detailed Federal or state regulations will be adopted to specify requirements for all of industry may well be determined by how many companies in the next two years move from boilerplate to significant action."

DOCTRINES AND PRINCIPLES

"The Reindustrialization of America." *Business Week,* June 30, 1980, pp. 55–142.

This special issue states the problem of the decline of U.S. industry and its causes, then offers a three-part solution that incorporates a new social contract, a policy for industry, and policies to spur investment and trade. The editors state: "Management for growth is possible." Companies ". . . can reaffirm the need for basic research, for taking risks, for planning for the long haul. And they can create a climate in which educated risk-takers feel that their jobs are secure and that their willingness to take risks is appreciated." They further state that since information has replaced goods ". . . the new information-based society cannot be gauged with the economic yardsticks formulated for the old world."

Index